T0196091

SHADES OF LIGHT, MIGHT, RIGHT AND INSIGHT!

JEFF FORMAN

BALBOA.
PRESS

A DIVISION OF HAY HOUSE

Balboa Press books may be ordered through booksellers or by contacting:

Balboa Press
A Division of Hay House
1663 Liberty Drive
Bloomington, IN 47403
www.balboapress.com
1 (877) 407-4847

Because of the dynamic nature of the Internet, any web addresses or
links contained in this book may have changed since publication and may
no longer be valid. The views expressed in this work are solely those
of the author and do not necessarily reflect the views of the publisher,
and the publisher hereby disclaims any responsibility for them.

The author of this book does not dispense medical advice or prescribe the use
of any technique as a form of treatment for physical, emotional, or medical
problems without the advice of a physician, either directly or indirectly. The
intent of the author is only to offer information of a general nature to help you
in your quest for emotional and spiritual well-being. In the event you use any
of the information in this book for yourself, which is your constitutional right,
the author and the publisher assume no responsibility for your actions.

Any people depicted in stock imagery provided by Getty Images are
models, and such images are being used for illustrative purposes only.
Certain stock imagery © Getty Images.

Print information available on the last page.

ISBN: 978-1-9822-1965-9 (sc)
ISBN: 978-1-9822-1967-3 (hc)
ISBN: 978-1-9822-1966-6 (e)

Library of Congress Control Number: 2019900744

Balboa Press rev. date: 11/18/2019

Contents

THE STRUGGLE

I trust you are thriving,
and not just surviving.
Are you one of the..s..e few?
who? know.s? or go.s?
along with their song,
whether or not most think it wrong?
Can it be deemed right?
through the might, of a few
who .. work out of sight,
and often at night,
alone in their plight
to fight
the unenlightened oppressors
and aggressors.

Can these purveyors
of ill-gotten behavior
            behave
in a fashion other than that of knaves
or are they
    slaves
of their knavery?
destined to rave on
In their depravity?

Must they lust
    and mistrust
      those with just intentions?
or can they dispense with the pretension?
Has our world entered a dimension

AN AUTUMN WONDER

The tree-tops glistened
The flowers listened
For morning had come anew.
The dew lay strewn
Like a silvery moon
And the sky was oh so blue!

And the birches lay
With shadows astray
But there were only a few.
The tall pines towered
But small flowers cowered
For they were far below.

The flowers bloomed
And the harsh wind crooned
For autumn was all aglow.
And the breeze was strong
But the flowers n'er gone
For nature whispered snow!

of intervention?
of different factions
bent on the detraction
of each other
voicing dissatisfaction
with one's brother
afraid to discover
another
alternative?

Well shove it!
I don't have to love it!
So leave it,
or else believe it
like a nit-wit,
full of shit!
I'm Hip!

What About You?

Conceived & Transmitted by Jeff Forman late pm/early am January 25th/26th, 1981 during my last year at college in Boulder, CO. Typed late pm 3/25/19 with text mirroring the way I hand-wrote it (which also included a notation I inserted above the last verse to Mom: Optional verse for the younger generation!) Included with a brief letter to my parents dated February 7th, 1981 in which I mention " Lastly, a couple of weeks ago I just all of a sudden started writing my first poem in a long time. Enclosed is a copy of what came out." Love, Jeff. ALL RIGHTS RESERVED.

DAYBREAK

The soft perfume, thy daisy's hair
The new born foal beside the mare
In quiet silence awaits the hare
For something to become aware.

In cold grey stillness
The forest shrouds
The gleaming mists
Above the clouds

Yet through the mists
A light doth break
Announcing thus
That dawn's awake!

THE BEAD GAME

Like beads found in a game of go
They appear all the same you know
Their subtleties abound yet glow
Not the least bit profound but so?!

Radiatingly implausible
Yet fashionably laudable
Attesting to conformity
Arresting uniformity.

Conceived @2:30-3 am on September 7th, 2002 for The "Bead Game" hobnail receptacle
for Scandleglass Creations for Enlightenment by Jeff Forman

CUT TO CLEAR RUBY

Elongated portals enriching inspection
As multiple flame points command eyes connection
To arrowheads pointing in heavens direction
Displaying ones yearnings for stellar conception!

Conceived 4:30-5:00 am, September 7th, 2002 except for the last line which was aptly tweaked into shape 12:37-12:38 am, December 2nd, 2010 for ruby cut to clear cigarette holder positioned on platter 2nd from top on Stand # 16 for Scandleglass Creations for Enlightenment by Jeff Forman

THE BEDAZZLER

Kaleidoscope pinwheels of dazzling wonder(s)
Mesmerizing eyes and casting thoughts asunder!
All points of perspective fully poised and balanced
Seducing one's conscious plane, stability renounced!

Crystalline optic spears like daggers projecting
Indelibly mirrored on pupil's reflecting
Betwixt boundaries unforeseen thus neglecting
To safely guard all those who warrant protecting!

Conceived and Transmitted by Jeff Forman @3-3:45 pm, October 23rd, 2002. ALL RIGHTS RESERVED.

"UN-REQUITED LOVE, BOTH RE-INSTILLED AND FINALLY FULL-FILLED"

Thus it was just so many years ago
A seed that was planted starting to grow
In the beginning when we first sensed it,
Slowly but surely it crept bit by bit
As though it was actually meant to be,
Despite the plain fact that we couldn't see
That there was a spark that kindled itself
Arcing between us our hearts bridged in stealth.

However its flame was quite delicate
Hence seemingly extinguished by fate,
It simmered lingering unacknowledged
Appearing to bid farewell on that date,
Hence more than a decade had now passed
As if it had been a forgotten bell
Whose toll had faded away in dismay?
To peel no more in withering decay.

But its resonance lingered on
As it echoed through the beyond,
Ever so softly until one fine day
It manifested itself once again
Both rekindled and fully renewed
Including a wholly fresh point of view
Having a holy new cyclic debut
In order to both instill and renew

The yet un-harvested love of two hearts
Linked once before but as yet unfulfilled
In storing away such delicate tenderness
Until a time when such hearts ached togetherness
Supposedly thwarted and parted but then
As two timid souls were stretched in such anguish
With fate intervening but yet once again
As they both soared high in limbo and languished

Henceforth thus waiting until that day came
When their pure spirits would rejoice again
At last now their longing in song and joined voice
Hearts before parted now jumpstarted by choice
Through their essence of re-mingled energies
No longer denied true fulfillment it seems
Until such a time when appropriately deemed

For both consummating and satiating their passionate love
Until relinquishing such joyous bonding to their essence above,
Thus recalling blissful oneness of achieved re-identity
Through their universal awareness and beginnings that they see!

Essence born and written in prose form early-mid afternoon on January 11, 2006 and
inspired by Susan Rill an old friend from West Palm Beach, Florida.
Re-worked and fleshed out becoming a poem begun in the late evening of July 25 and
finished on the morning of July 26, 2009 by about 4 am. by Jeff F. Forman.

AND SO REDEMPTION ANEW, AS WE RECLAIM HONOR TOO

So I know we're all going to get the truth,
Hearken to the angels singing out anew!
As the universe (w)rings out it's cosmic sleuths
To expedite bringing home the troops.
Thus saving us all our precious youth,
And reuniting us as a group
Of spiritual beings born on earth
Endowed with the rights of humane birth.

And those who don't yield
From their downtrodding ways,
To enable us realizing
Our God given claims,
Will be trampled themselves
So don't be dismayed!

For our fathers of fortune
And our mothers of spirit
Enacted intentions well proportioned,
So let the divine feminine clear it!
Thus we may all then begin anew
To (re)appreciate the cosmic view!

Conceived by Jeff Forman on June 10th & 11th, 2007

USING RESOURCE TO GET BACK ON COURSE FROM YOUR OWN SOURCE

You can run away and hide, thus staying afraid
Not daring to face yourself for (yet) another day,
Or you can vault that great divide and bridge
That gap of division and indecision within your self
So on this and each and every new day henceforth
You not just yearn but learn to embrace your own wealth

Thus molding a new you with your being unified
And forging together a new found armor aligned
Blending all of the seemingly discombobulated,
Disoriented, detached facets incarcerated
Within the new found self, in order to reap the wealth
That your soul itself has previously been denied,
As the child within has hidden in stealth,
Not daring to fully share itself in mild dismay
And embrace that sometimes wild ride of each and every brand new day.

Yet what a thrill to but just re-instill that sense of truly immense
Power of purpose that may have also been on forced holiday,
Where your great dismay from trials and tribulations once again
Caused your child to run and hide and lock away
The key to your future destiny,
That insecure and shy chagrined part of yourself that you've unwittingly
Ostracized and imprisoned within that lonely tower you've built
Bereft of wealth and sustenance, allowing it to conveniently cower in guilt

And thus cover its face from others and the rest of (the whole) itself
Content to be a fragment that looks out and about, from time to time yearning
For friends, when all that is needed is quite simply learning
To turn the corner and reflect within, that that which has been imprisoned without
And locked from its sense of purpose, thus up until now in doubt,
Can re-assign and re-align its self, and re-unite its prior oneness instilling wealth,
Thus forging and finding the wholeness that comes from pruning
The strands and shards of apparent alienation, dissention and division, and grooming
Them, to not only face but embrace a once lost but newly found sense of unification,
Unity and cohesion, cementing in place once more as you connect with the core
Of that big blueprint that's been temporarily hidden away in dismay
Apparently on a misguided proverbial holiday.

Yet all one needs to do is unlock that dusty room of refuge
With that rediscovered key to fully re-embrace humanity
As the re-united whole new you, back from your blues with your chinks fused
And those stragglers re-entwined, as they've been re-defined and re-aligned
With their essential DNA, to once again run and play in cheer without fear,
Knowing that this newly found oneness within, can be manifested and embraced without
No longer allowing a few bruises and blues to fragment oneself from itself in doubt
Thus embracing and loving each and every facet of yourself
Knowing for the first time and finally believing
That the true you can never be blue for longer than it takes

To feel one's feet firmly planted, thus rooted in touch with mother earth
Content in the innate stability, oneness and wholeness grounded to one's self worth!

Written during a hot news flash fired from the divine
Transmitted through my high self and inspired to define
Standing within the naked truth of my own birthday suit
Stripped bare of my nightly attire, undressed and not yet groomed
For this new day, cultivating a few goose bumps along the way
As I'm compelled to write this witty little ditty filled with insight,
Before any more of a chill can instill a different kind of cool,
That comes from standing all of this time at my kitchen counter like a fool
Bereft of covering, content nonetheless in the success of nothing less
Than writing this, and hopefully both enticing and inciting I profess
Another way to re-connect each and every day with one's DNA.

Conceived by Jeff F. Forman on January 31, 2009
Re-written with slight revisions on February 8 & 9, and finally on June 14, 2009.

Inspired by Sheryl Richards, this is for her, me, and any and all other human beings who have in some way been fragmented by the traumas of divine incarnation and/or the insensitivity of their fellow man. J.F.F.

CHESSMEN

As the chessmen stand within their own spaces
All occupying their respective places
Some with solemn countenance etched upon their faces
Others exude status based upon their social graces

Soon to move from their home squares
Some as designated pairs
With which like countenance is shared
In hopes they will be well prepared

Venturing forth thus to engage
Perhaps opponents full of rage
Best not bereft of proper sage
Sagas not reached their final page
At least before a timely age

Some are valiant, some less pure
Of stalwart heart to still endure
The battle scars of dreaded foes
Succumbing from respective blows
Resulting from those seeds they'd sowed

Traversing paths of great insight
Not bowing to superior might
Nor wallowing in petty spite
Preferring not to turn in flight
Determined not to yield to fright

As the skirmishes wind down
One king's eventually struck down
Its army finally yields its crown
Perhaps in defeat wearing frowns
All countenances tilted down
No longer whole in heart and sound
No courage left yet to be found
With vanquished colleagues on the ground.

Initially conceived on June 14th, 2010 for Stands #22 & #29 for Scandleglass Creations for Enlightenment by Jeff Forman and subsequently tweaked with minor revisions + the last 2 lines added on September 25th, 2011 from 12:50-2:30 am.

SWIRLS OF OPALESCENCE

Swirls of red and white and blue
When loving opalescence too
Just might make your dreams come true
Sending thrills and chills through you!

While feasting one's eyes in rapt attention
Holding one's breath in sudden suspension
No idle thoughts to cause intervention
(Just) Blissful wonder imposing detention.

Poem #1 from August 29th, 2010 @ noon conceived for stand #74? for Scandleglass Creations for Enlightenment by Jeff Forman

I SPY WITH MY LITTLE EYE

Hobnails of various shapes and sizes
A treasure trove of endless surprises
Like a selection of wonderful prizes
Continually widening ones eyeses!

Poem #2 from August 29th, 2010 @ 12:30 pm conceived for Stand # 45 for Scandleglass
Creations for Enlightenment by Jeff Forman

THE NATURE OF OWLS

Perched on their branches in rapt attention
Like palace guards displaying convention
All movement held in total suspension
A lifetime of disciplined retention
Waiting for time to cause intervention

The hare below displaying no care
In timeless bliss requiring no prayer
Minding his business quite unaware
Soon to sense horror before his despair
Back to the essence that all creatures share.

Poem #3 from August 29th 2010 @ 12:50-1:12 pm & finished at 3:10-3:13 pm conceived for Stand #1 for Scandleglass Creations for Enlightenment by Jeff Forman

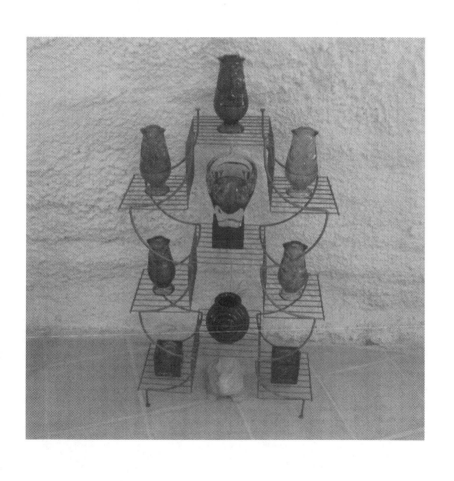

THE CUT TO CLEAR
CLASS OF GLASS

Circles, sprigs, twigs with escalloped bases
Symmetrically ringed with perfect spaces
All etched within their respective places
Aptly adorned eliciting praises
Mostly small rose bowls but two bud vases
And one boasts stars that finely encase it
Candles within boast beauty and graces
Our eyes alight with enraptured faces!

Poem # 4 from August 29th, 2010 @2-2:28 pm conceived for Stand #35 for Scandleglass
Creations for Enlightenment by Jeff Forman

ART DECO DELIGHTS

Five beauteous vases adorn this stand
Its contrasting black looks oh so grand
Scrollwork so fine so let's strike up the band
Eliciting but one simple command
For our eyes to only barely withstand
No finer feasts for them in all the land.

Poem #5 August 29th, 2010 @ 2:30-3 pm conceived for Stand #31 for Scandleglass
Creations for Enlightenment by Jeff Forman
This stand which inspired this poem is pictured on the front and back cover of the book.

UNITY

Unity unites both one and all
So that together we all stand tall
Answering to our unified call
Much less likely allowing a fall
From grace into a separate place
Where we just might embrace such disgrace
As to fester within our own space
Thus some dividing the human race
Content to divide and deride each other
Even allowing our spirits to smother
When the going gets tough running for cover
Instead (of) allowing ourselves to recover
That sense of shame to get back in the game
And realize that we're all one and the same
Sourced from the divine from whence we all came
Knowing together we can all regain
Our exalted essence which all can retain!

Poem # 6 on August 29th, 2010 @3:33-4 pm and further tweaked on December 3rd, 2010 @ 1:35-2:05 am initially conceived for Stand #73 UNITY for Scandleglass Creations For Enlightenment by Jeff Forman

A HOBNAIL CHRISTMAS TREE

Come one come all so you can see
A wondrous hobnail Christmas tree
That's all decked out inspiring glee
All standing firm yet fancy free

Its arms stretched out with numerous colors
In varying hues and some like brothers
Yet all quite unlike any others
With none need hiding under covers*

A potpourri of shapes and sizes
Like a feast of coveted prizes
Resplendent and in many guises
Ever unveiling new surprises*

When sunbeams bathe each with its light
All eyes transfixed alight with sight
No mortal could summon the might
To even try to turn take flight
No reason to put up a fight
For all agree their gaze is right

And when dusk falls and shadows loom
Across the floor into the room
There's no submission to the gloom
Nor reason to encourage doom
Each holder hosts a new born bloom
As candles lit rekindle plumes

Despite the fading of the day
No disappointment come what may
Each holder hosts its own array
Of circles vast in fine display

Encouraging ones further stay
Engaging orbs to further play
No thoughts at all to turn away
As cycle repeats each new day.

Conceived @2:08-3:18 am September 4th, 2010 with 2 lines* added 12:48-12:53 am December 4th, 2010 for stand #51 for Scandleglass Creations for Enlightenment by Jeff Forman

A THANKSGIVING PLEDGE FOR FUTURE REALIZED NOW

As the year two thousand ten winds down
May all good men and women be found
To reap rewards and have good reason
Throughout this coming New Year season
The more their blessings will abound
The more their joyous hearts resound
As fewer tears will hit the ground
When brotherhood of man's re-found

No longer left still cloaked in stealth
Not only focused on oneself
Instead promoting all towards wealth
A new found universal health!

Abolishing the need for fear
With mind's eye seeing very clear
Now joy will reign throughout the year
Resultant in abundant cheer

Now humankind as one worldwide
With none left out to be denied
And none so shallow to deride
No reason left for one to hide
All countenances full of pride
As mankind reigns supreme worldwide!

Seeded early am November 19th, 2010 & conceived 6:15-6:45 pm November 20th, 2010
by Jeff Forman

CATTAILS FOR YOU TOO

Cattails for two or three or four
Located just inside my front door
The fourth with a spot upon the floor
Not so inopportune to ignore
Nor likely to inspire a snore
Or perish the thought become a bore!

While flanked with two swans on either side
Both loyal enough indeed to abide
Content for now they relinquish glide
One with head raised in eminent pride
To such lofty heights they now reside
All realizing naughts left to be decried

None so brazen enough to deride
No longer reaping thoughts to collide
Nor sowing seeds derisively wide
Thus compelling some meek to hide
No longer in stealth should one confide
Waking humanity now unified!

Initially conceived for Stand #57 for Scandleglass Creations for Enlightenment on December 22nd, 2010 @ 4:20-5:10 am by Jeff Forman

COMMISSIONED VISIONARIES

Those people with vision
Who make right decisions
With proper conditions
Are aptly commissioned
By those of just mission
On acts of attrition
Perhaps snide derision
Even abolition
Fie those seed division
For truth has arisen!

Bringing fear to a halt
Banishing all assault
Using proper gestalt
Leaping over all faults
None too large to not vault
Cleansing wounds with some salt
Wisdom no longer stalt

No more wars to be fought
No more souls left distraught
Victim's nerves now not fraught
Vices no longer sought
No one still can be bought
Weakened will now be naught
All malice has been caught
For real joy has been brought
As goodness has been taught
From those of highest thought!

Verse 1 conceived on February 2nd, 2011 @6:45-7:10 am and 2 & 3 @8:15-8:55 am by Jeff Forman

FEAST OR FAMINE, REASON OR MADNESS, BANISH SADNESS AND AWAKEN TO GLADNESS!

As two thousand eleven is almost passed by
Having caused humans too many sights for sore eyes
Enduring much pain yielding prolific outcries
For many oppressed by the tyranny will die
And two thousand twelve looms ever soon to be nigh
Will it actually soon become twelve o'clock high?!

As the wars of greed and madness
Rage further along in the East
Some ponder with detached sadness
As others prepare for the feast
Of famine they unleash their beast
In blindly courting false gladness

Oblivious to their own downfall
Must maintain the proper protocol
Continue to stifle and forestall
Both troops and reason denied recall
Plummeting lives blissfully in freefall
Padding their pockets thus standing tall!?
How soon will this false sense of enthrall
Be shook off or detached from their ball?!

Will their relentless march to doom be derailed?
Before more poor souls are entombed and assailed?
Instead may they find (their) false aspirations failed
As greater humanity awakens prevailed!

In their unison smiting their own ugly beast
Which society spawned as a plague thus unleashed
Steadfast in denial with compassion breached
Assailing each other all reason impeached!

Others awaken in shocking disbelief
Far from enabled to sacrifice their grief
Unto the false leaders they once hailed as chiefs
Now seen from their shorn state as victimized sheep
Fleeced of their prosperity the price is steep
Cushioning the castles their oppressors keep
Can their skin or pockets really be that deep?!
Or will they awaken unto their own thief's!
Thus reclaiming truth's universal belief
And restoring honor as vital to keep!

Conceived by Jeff Forman @ 1:30-3:55am on December 9th, 2011 with the last line added 4:15-4:30 pm.

FOCUS ON THE LIGHT

Focus on the light
Don't let it get out of sight!
If necessary use all your might
And never succumb to fright
Nor allow yourself to take flight!

Instead use your own insight
And unlock your key to delight!
Thus transforming prior plights
Into wisps of fading nights
As the sun shines ever so bright
making everything quite alright!

Conceived and Transmitted by Jeff Forman from 4:35-4:38 am on January 15th, 2012.
Last line #5 of verse 1 added at 11:58 pm on February 6th, 2012. ALL RIGHTS RESERVED.

THE WONDERS OF STEIFF

Those stuffed toys lovingly made by Steiff
Which so charmingly animate life
And alleviate young children's strife
Even when lying awake at night
Perhaps from a nightmare's awful plight
With the timing just barely all right
Acting upon intuitive insight
Delivering innocents from their fright
With eyes wide open shining quite bright
Illuminated from the lamp's light
Transformed from fearful back to delight!

Conceived by Jeff Forman @ 5:25-5:40 am February 10th,2012 with last line added @11:34 pm 3/1/12

AWAKENING (TO DESTINY)

Barrack Obama took an oath of office, the highest in our land
In order to faithfully serve the people and take a noble stand
Whether twas to represent all or a select few within his band
His fancy rhetoric dazzled many as he said yes we can
Enable change for good of one and all for every woman and man
Yet his actions have proven largely empty with words like shifting sand
Despite such bold attempts to pass himself off as such an erudite man
In final judgement will it mean the ultimate end to his whole clan?!

He brings to mind another tale of one so pompously inflated
That had no limits to his taste for (greed and) power so falsely elated
As history has recorded there have been many before him slated
That proudly rose to dizzying heights, their evil appetites never satiated
Eventually their false delusions expire as many offended berated
Realizing that no longer can this falsehood render them placated
And sadly once again a charlatan's destroyed what could have been created.

He said he stood for change and truth to render governing more transparent
Yet now his actions clearly show that the opposites quite apparent
He occupies his office dictating orders like a giant
To anyone that questions motives he becomes quite defiant
And sends his minions to invoke wrath on any not compliant
Has anyone not yet seen the mantle he's adopted as a tyrant?!

Once again some fairy tales most aptly convey both to one and all
How Humpty Dumpty inflated himself leering down from his high wall
Never once fearing that his kingdom could all come crashing down and fall
Thinking that it was sufficient to just curry his delusional call
Consumed with his own stature as his servants celebrated their ball
Whilst oppression grew amongst many igniting anger into brawls.

Still blindly like the emperor he's enchanted with his own image
Just like a foolish football team rehearsing another scrimmage
His wife shares in her own appetites also lacking real foresight
Reveling in new gowns and clothes bathing herself in the spotlight(s)
Never thinking much for those commoners immersed in her delight
Whilst more people awaken to the truth no longer bereft of sight.

No longer able to be fooled or beguiled with such false cloaks
Their nakedness now quite apparent, their falsehood like black smoke
As the entire country and many people become ever more broke
Yet the tyranny continues in their persistence to deny truth to all folk(s)
All that will soon come crashing down as God's wrath will invoke
Turning the tide towards truth and justice restoring humanity's hope
So we'll all unite across the earth and answer false oppression with nope!
We don't want it, we won't take it, we can't stand you anymore!
We're not going to be like so many in the past just groveling on the floor
Instead we're collectively on board to send you out the door
We've had enough false promises that only yield more poor!

But pity those who've not yet seen the truth as they still slumber
And don't stumble into thinking that they just must be much dumber
Nor feel that they hold back progress and through denial thus encumber
Nor succumb to such temptation to whack those dullards heads awake with lumber
Instead see them as all in essence as your own sisters and your brothers
No matter what race, creed or countries, love them purely as one another
So that more and more evolve in consciousness thus to discover
That no longer can false politicians continue to smite and smother
True awareness that when ignited will have them all running for cover
Their nakedness now on display for all to plainly see
Their moribund souls bereft of honor and accountability
Reclaiming all the people's rights to truth and honesty
Restoring all humanity to prosperity through responsibility.

And fie to those who blindly yield to slavery and servitude
Or languish in such cushy jobs content in their ineptitude
Such flagrant disrespect for others brazen in their attitudes
Content continuing dishing out so many false platitudes
So lacking in humility, how can they be so bloody crude?!
How long must the rest of us endure them being so outright rude!?
Only as long as it takes until enough unite thus to diffuse
These false purveyors wielding power who continue to abuse
Contented to usurp those less reasoned continuing to confuse
Those who foolishly think they're being told the truth through local news
Until they can no longer spread malicious lies subverting truth
No longer dooming future generations of our precious youth.

Their tenure's already on the wane as they scramble to deceive
Their misguided efforts will prove in vain denied to them achieve
As in the past all evil empires can't possibly conceive
As they crumble in the dust along with those who falsely believed
Struck down by God's pure judgement despite man's temporary
reprieve.

Conceived by Jeff Forman @ 10:10am-1:10pm on Feb.27th2012 & edited 12:20-4:10am
March 2nd 2012

TRANSFORMATION

May greater humanity soon take heed
That it's very survival can now proceed
By purging those tainted content to deceive
Their negative karma will soon be received
Perhaps no longer enabled to breed
If they can't spread (their) diabolical seed
That continues subverting man's greater need(s)
For a healthy society to succeed
In turn rewarding greater men's noble deeds
Restoring truths fundamentally based creed!

As vital to mans higher resonation
In his eternal quest for salvation
No longer yielding only deprivation
Instead now fulfilling inherent destination
Perhaps by virtue of God's prestidigitation
Ably assisted by mankind's amalgamation
Much due to her re-awakened excitation
In restoring zeal as the key to elation
Knowing no one's left to seed consternation
The final component for man's healthful transformation!

Conceived by Jeff Forman on June 9th, 2012 between 3:36 & 5:06 am with minor tweaking on June 12th.

42

FROM CROWN TO COMMONWEALTH

Will they all end up soon being?
Architects of their own demise
Steadfast in not seeing
As their war drums beat reprise
Never quite within their hearing
The abject collective human cries
Reverberating, Yet never fearing
The portents their karma decries

Their callousness diffuses knowing
Thus it comes as no surprise
That they also negate growing
Except when infusing material wealth
Incessantly, as they've continued sowing
Their tyrannical seeds in stealth
Unwittingly promoting humanity's awakening
As they've pummeled its collective health!

If only instead they'd cultivated enabling
And renounce(d) their selfish ways to history's bygone shelf
(In turn) rekindling the light of truth thus saving
And causing their hardened hearts to melt
In return cultivating and now subsequently gracing
New historic annals resplendent as a wholehearted commonwealth
Emerging and quickly evolving and replacing
Past aggressions transformed now compassionately heartfelt!

Conceived by Jeff Forman 2:45-3:40 am, July 5th,2012. Typed & tweaked 5:40-6:30 pm July 10th,2012.

(THE ILLUSION OF)
PARTISAN POLITICS

Things are heating up with all of the four year national conventions
That historically manages to rivet much of the public's attention
Despite all of the histrionics and staged bogus false pretention
What will be the major coverage that the media chooses to mention?!
Regardless of it all these false forums will still yield NO redemption
When the current puppet oppressor can dictate any unlimited detention
Based on whatever his maniacal handlers implement as 'just' prevention
To protect us all from the bogey man that's clearly their invention
To nullify and brainwash all they can from their own true intentions!

And will the response be one of overall praise or lamentation
Voiced by a large percentage of our fine nation's population?
Well often that depends upon perception and discernment
And when they believe so fervently that their success is imminent
They revel and cheer wildly in a massive orgy of contentment
As they feel ever emboldened and empowered in shared element
Often qualifying prior slander as equally justifiable resentment
This pillar of party politics that draws such strong commitment
Inspires all players to reveal their cores as bickering immature adolescents!

So how can it be they all perceive themselves so radically different?!
Have you not yet seen behind the(ir) sheen of illusion and pretention?!
That they've managed to uphold for decades of delusion and division
Effectively nullifying any real change through constricted convictions
Inflicted upon many honorable but still gullible naturalized citizens

Quite a few of whom still desperately rigidly cling to their partisan politics
So steadfastly loyal to supporting a bunch of pumped up adolescent pricks!
Who are becoming ever more depraved in their petty party antics
Sensing the crumbling mortar holding their parties foundations bricks
All the more reason they now resort to the lowest and vilest tricks
To retain this dwindling smokescreen and their ever bigger sticks
That they've wielded so effectively in making and keeping people sick
By conning many into believing that all ills have been duly inflicted
By that 'other' incompetent party and its partisan politics so kindly gifted!
As more now each day navigate through all the cons and lies successfully sifted
Gleaning truth after decades of lies and falsehoods with smokescreens effectively lifted!

Conceived & transmitted by Jeff Forman @3:20-5:15 am on August 30th/2012 with lines 5-9 added & additional tweaking from @ 4:20-6:05 pm

FROM OPPRESSION TO NATURAL SELECTION

Since the dawn of time the earth has spawned countless civilizations
Some were small having little clout while some grew into nations
And when they lasted for awhile each formed their own delegations
This in turn ensured the further growth of certain manifestations
Which in turn attracted other folks who forumed into congregations
Each was intent upon garnering favor with various implementations
That attracted and inducted others accepting this form of representation
Always groomed in converting any outstanding members of the population
As well as absorbing opposing disconsolate factions into their amalgamations
Never shy in promoting any new form of manipulative legislation
Inevitably cloaked within some form of enacted restrictive regulations
Always intent upon staging the most outlandish supportive presentations
Never concerned with how damaging or falsely projected their insinuations
Nor the fallout from failed policies implemented bearing huge ramifications!

Intent upon their singular agenda(s) enabling yet more indoctrination
To best achieve this one world order make policy mirror personification
In turn intent upon no longer allowing any further individual contemplation
Especially those who might dare promote truth thus soiling their reputations

And by any and all means suppress all who might stage confrontations!

For allowing any alternative views just might result in some defection
That could require down the road unpleasant forms of stifling correction
Often resulting in some kind of subtly limiting forms of inspection
Thrust upon the general population guised to benefit their protection
The recently empowered TSA debasing us all with its immoral injection!
And woe to any who oppose or resist by voicing their rejection
For now if one so boldly chooses to enact free wills deflection
The United Kingdom deems that grounds for any flyers ejection
Does that not give any sane humans cause for serious reflection?
That any country can categorically dictate such restrictions sans election
Put forth enshackling truth and freedom with perverse false projection!
And yet another society's ensuring decaying morals resurrection
Are all of us so damnably complacent in assuring its natural selection?
Or will it stir enough awakened precipitating mass convection
Thus overthrowing another civilizations decay from gross oppression
Just in time to restore our moral fabric thus saving humanity's direction!

Partial seeding of 2nd verse Sept. 7th 2012. Conceived by Jeff Forman @ 1:00am-3:45am Sept. 8th, 2012.
Typed and tweaked with minor revisions from 11:48pm Sept. 8th-1:10am September 9th, 2012

A MORAL COMPASS REINSTATED

In the beginning both scholars and historians have all maintained and frequently stated
Various opinions of conjecture as to whence and how man evolved or was created
Despite their own cultures preponderance to accept their proponents' theories well dated
And in turn be prone to pridefully profess that theirs was the first to be officially slated
As well as maintaining quite adamantly that all others reports were (only) just duplicated
Or perish the thought maybe them being resultant from spies thus appropriated!
Rather than allowing adequate humility to arise and admit that other cultures also related
Both annals and stories from similar eras that realistically must be associated
(Thus) accepting such broader enabling views ensuring that all were duly initiated
Nor succumbing to such arrogant views that all other pretenders must be soundly berated!
And allowing this false pride to fester and grow in turn rendering them thus placated
Ensuring their society's own devolution to eventually becoming ever more emaciated
The end result of such self immolation rendering their culture more swiftly terminated!
As their own blindness to allowing all others independence of thought to be aptly appreciated
Instead promoting a subtle form of mass hypnosis via indoctrination ever more regulated

Which can often devolve culture into what appears to be superficially amalgamated

No consideration given to the possibilities of greater truths being totally obfuscated

For those who question this direction's imminently hazardous path so falsely paraded

Must be singled out and vilified as ones to be ostracized or at the very least relegated

Or perhaps just reduced to public disgrace by a slanderous media (and) thus humiliated

Or even worse them being branded imbalanced thus requiring them being incarcerated

This effectively negates their personage, all rights to free speech being obliterated!

As others freely succumb to Big Pharma's aplomb thus rendering themselves sedated

An even more heinous fate of some tortured souls being subsequently permanently negated

The worst travesties escalating to such demonic levels as genocide with everyone annihilated

Not for one moment realizing that such tyranny itself must only become duly devastated

Nor quelling their perverted lust for power and greed thus rendering its term(s) abbreviated

Instead continuing to court catastrophe dooming all with false doctrines once again regurgitated

As every tyrant throughout history has groomed his greed and power so pompously inflated

From kingdom come to oblivion control and madness manifest with further edicts dictated

Seeding mass consternation causing many displaced from their homes as forcefully migrated

Does any sane mortal not truly recognize the terminal folly that's being precipitated?

For those who perceive history's casualties of cultures gone astray neither transformed nor abated

Instead continuing Hell bent on perilous paths rendering all false prophets and followers cremated

And through distortion of God and religion allowing the travesties of Alexandria's truths incinerated

Instead they should have wisely adopted policies encouraging truth not banished but elevated

As the fundamental staff of life and light thus rendering all cultures equally invigorated

Ensuring a new civilization for all of mankind where enlightenment's both worshipped and traded

Thus restoring a long lost and elusive status quo where everyone's souls are constantly elated

As the end of all oppression, archaic wars and human conflict are forevermore celebrated

Promoting truth with free speech everywhere on earth and beyond no matter where congregated

As all shackle their own egomaniacal tendencies allowing joy worldwide to never become satiated

No longer promoting and allowing the disease of their dark sides to become so falsely validated

Rendering such past perversions to nothing more than historical footnotes forever antiquated

With planet earth and all of its dwellers embracing equal rights and status forever emancipated

Thus once and for all ensuring humanity's flourishing with everyone's moral compasses reinstated!

Substantial seeding 12:22-12:27 am on September 9th, 2012. Initially conceived & fleshed out by Jeff Forman on September 24th 10:50 pm-1:00 am Sept. 25th, 2012 with 2nd last line subsequently becoming 4th last added @1:20 am. Typed out with further tweaking and additional seeding yielding the additions of lines 23-25, 27-35, 39-41 and 44 & 45 from @ 3:20-9:25 pm. ALL RIGHTS RESERVED. Jeff Forman

THE CO-DEPENDENCE TRAP

With countenance bolstered up and out
You're tempted to emit a shout
Another host to boast about
Instead of building your OWN clout
Still yet fostering your own pout
Succumbing to just another lout
Who's not about to let YOU out
Instead propping up your own self doubt
And pumping himself ever more stout
As both retain NO gain within bereft without!

Conceived by Jeff Forman @ 5:05-5:25 am Sept. 13th,2012. Typed & tweaked 10:34-11:04 pm Sept.14th.
Inspired just after reading the final chapter of "UFOs and the Nature of Reality" by Judi Pope Koteen and Dedicated to Sheryl Richards and any and all other individuals who unwittingly submit their free will & spirit to those who like to feed their own image with the false apparent power of domination of others. May they soon find their own inner strength to break the shackles that they allow to bind them and in so doing reclaim their own equality of self expression.

GREED—A SEED ONCE PLANTED

The need for greed not recanted
Fulfilled desire(s) not supplanted
Instead perverted as fame drains
It stains the soul and sucks it dry
A brief and subsequently bitter high
Distorted reason left to die
All sense of truth left withering nigh
As barren lands beneath the sky.

Once full of life with mind's eye clear
Vanquishing all that was once held dear
What a high price paid for such vapid cheer
Like an addict's fix, a brutal mix
It sucks the life creating strife
Along the way cuts like a knife
Confusing temperance blinding insight
Cheap thrills replacing true delight
Which flowed once freely ever bright?
Now yielding endless nights through plights
No longer able to see the light.

The spark of truth forever dimming
Vitality drained through constant trimming
Instead of surging fulfilled and brimming
A witch's brew trapped in whirlpools swimming
Distorted will held in a vice
A gambler's continual throw of the dice
Trapped in a maze like forlorn mice
Doomed to paying such a grievous price
It may eventually cost them their life!

Unless somehow they can diffuse
Their tendencies to self abuse
Admitting themselves (that) they lit the fuse
To revel wildly and recklessly use
Their fellow humans selfishly singed
Through their constant cruel eternal binge
That fueled the fires of funeral pyres
The acrid smoke from trashed hopes
The hangman's noose like a tightening rope
Not yet perceiving that they're the dope!

Caught in a trap of their own making
Instead of giving forever taking
Their consciences trapped shallowly placating
Until inevitably somehow breaking
Through the fog restoring clarity
Gaining humbleness through redeemed charity
Restoring righteousness through reason
Springing forth like a new season
Flowing like a river teaming
With new life and vitality streaming
Further and farther with souls now gleaming
Purged of scheming; now wondrously dreaming!

Conceived by Jeff Forman @11:38 pm-12:30 am May 1st - 2nd, 2014 with last line added @ 12:45 am.
Spontaneously inspired from & expediently written in free flow during a break in viewing the film Tulsa (1949) which depicted the heroine Susan Hayward succumbing to greedily lusting for installing more wells despite the pleas for temperance & preservation of the land from her Indian relative.

A PURGING OF GREATER HUMANITY

Within conflicts of epic scale
May cooler heads yet prevail
And common sense soon entail
That humanity (will) not fail
By casting (yet) another nail
In its own extinction trail.

Lost to all sense of reason
Inflicting multiple counts of treason
Via pathologic states of delusion
A chaotic new world illusion?!!
With a massive illegal's immoral infusion
Another patriotic exclusion intrusion
To what ends and contrived conclusion?!!

Destroy a once proud nation
A power mad emphatuation
No need for contemplation
Just reap false adulation
From a hoodwinked population
Full of useless information
Fattened on false legislation
Ear marked for concentration
On perverse propagandic persuasion
A necessary dire invasion
What? No consternation?!!

Rekindling steadfast resolve
Aggressions sanctfully solved
Dilemmas effectively dissolved
Enabling a new species evolved!

No longer prone to confuse
Instead inclined to enthuse
With more goodwill to infuse
All temptations now diffused
With malice effectively excused
Completely renounced and refused
No longer allowed nor abused.

Abhorred as an outright profanity
Purging greater humanity
Saving it from its (own) insanity
Promoting its prolific proclivity
Restoring its divine divinity
From trinity to inspired infinity!

No longer just a quaint notion
Inspired through intense promotion
Evoked with enriched enhanced emotion
Bolstered with such devout devotion
Diffusing all of that confusing commotion
Forging a sacrosanct locomotion in motion!

Conceived & transmitted by Jeff Forman @6:11-7:25 am on July 28th,2014 with line 36
added @7:33 am, lines 42-45 added @8:15-8:19 am + line 46 added@ 3:45 pm & line
47 added @ 3:55 pm.

POLITICS: THE ACHILLES HEEL OF HUMANITY

Lower than slimy slugs
Mentalities of vile thugs
Afflicting humanity like perpetual bugs
Disabling sanity like debilitating drugs!

False attention commanded
Perceptions appropriately sanded
With all reason supplanted
Accountability NOT demanded
The masses ever enchanted
Instead of feet firmly planted
Like astronauts successfully landed
Remaining castoffs forever stranded.

Trapped in netherworlds of illusion
Held perplexed within false infusions
Daily doses of dire intrusion
Diverting clarity, supporting delusions!

These predatory perpetual pill poppers
Obsessed with greedily enriching their coffers
While spiritually being no more than paupers
Running rampant sans legislative stoppers
Seemingly immune to all of the coppers
Many who also appear off their rockers!
Nothing more than power mad stalkers
Blinded like all egomaniacal talkers
They must be forcibly promoted as walkers!

Perceived clearly now as stacked deck players!
No longer accepted as truthful relayers
Discerned and dismissed as negative naysayers
Effectively denounced as false purveyors
Appropriately renounced as useless surveyors!

Who've strip-mined humanity in a played out vein
Have you not yet discerned their evil game?
As they arrogantly flaunt their (own) fame
In continual quest(s) to support their (vile) reign
All artfully crafted to enhance their (own) gain
Selfishly lurking behind their disdain
Unleashing torrents of afflicting rain
With stifling legislation ever more vain
Without thoughts given for this growing stain
Pummeling humanity, so bloody inhumane!
Only enabled by those truly insane!

It's high time right now to voice objection(s)
Supported with the required inflection(s)
Through renewed penetrating perception(s)
Disarming all perverted projection(s)
Renouncing all the sugary confection(s)
Diffusing all distorted deception(s)
Enabling all essential correction(s)
Automating constant appropriate deflection(s)
Empowering a massive defection
Implementing a healthy direction
Inoculating all false infection(s)
Leaving none behind with no exception(s)
A full-fledged spiritual resurrection!

Conceived & transmitted by Jeff Forman @ 2:30-5:15 pm on August 6th 2014 with some line ending rhyming words seeded as follows: lines 5,7,8,9 & 11 @ 12:20 pm on September 10th 2012; lines 17-20 @ 1:07 pm on September 11th 2012; lines 42,44,45 & 47-54 @ 11:40 am on 9/25/12. Line 26 was added @ 1:45pm on August 8th 2014. All Rights Reserved.

ABUNDANCE + EQUALITY
= UNIVERSAL BALANCE

Advancement yielding a new dimension
Entrancement renounced with renewed attention
No longer attached to feeble pretention
Deception detached from outright duplicion
Seen clearly now as a massive affliction
All reception restored with utter conviction
Innate convection enhancing eviction
A thorough ejection of all superstition
Robust rejection of those under suspicion
Automatic deflection of any commissions
Deemed subversive or on harmful missions
By those repulsive disingenuous editions
Ever so impulsive to be known as politicians!
Anxiously compulsive in their edictal predictions
Artfully dismissive of their own derelictions
Coyly submissive maintaining conditions
Vindictive to all to promote their addictions!

Maintaining them passive through artful depletion
With superfluous rhetoric and petty persuasion
Always conducive to limiting equations
All rights renounced by such dire invasions
With free will trounced by such crafty creations
Which we must all denounce as vile aberrations
Relegated forever as bygone mutations!

Certainly never at all premature
The only way to really ensure
An overwhelming viable cure
That humanity simply must endure
To restore its vital essence pure
(Is) by renouncing all petty frivolity
That threatens any steadfast equality
(In) embracing only abundance for all
Thereby preventing humanity's fall
Struck down from God's grace into utter disgrace
An appropriate epitaph for our maligned race?!
Is it not yet too late for us to save face?
(By) collectively realigning ourselves with space
Restoring our divine selves (once again) in place
Promoting only that yielding abundance
Through equality achieving a universal balance!

Conceived & transmitted by Jeff Forman @ 11:45 pm August 28th-2:45 am August 29th, 2014 after substantial word seeding from 11:20-11:40 pm on August 28th. ALL RIGHTS RESERVED. Additional tweaking on December 4th with lines 21 & 22 conceived @ 9:59-10:05 pm & line 38 added by 11:59 pm.

ANIMALS IN THE ZOO

All children love to go to the zoo
Gleeful to see all the animals there and it's true
And if you ask them where they want to go to?
They'll chortle in unison "we want to go to the zoo, yes we do"!

But where they innocently choose to see comedy
A wiser soul acknowledges the real tragedy
All stripped of their essence and natural majesty!

As all animals, birds and fish thus confined
Within limited spaces duly defined
Lifetimes within these eternal confines
Punishment likewise (should be) befitting such crimes
Truly contemptible they should end for all time!

If only we could facilitate an adequate cure
To put a final end to what such creatures must endure!

Conceived & transmitted by Jeff Forman @ 7:52-8:25 pm on October 4th 2014. All Rights Reserved.
Inspired in free flow after watching the first few minutes of Dick Powell's Four Star Playhouse #7 The Officer and The Lady 12/18/52.

THE FALSE NOBILITY OF TRADITIONAL ROYALTY

Many (wo)men play different roles
And in so doing some sell their souls
Others act in the shadows as moles
Or perpetrate acts of cruelty as trolls
Never pondering that such behavior
Disingenuous in design to curry favor
So artfully crafted as petty enablers
Will not result as their own soul's savior!

An errant game of false projections
Perpetually played as interjections
Foisted upon (the) masses sans rejection
Many of whom are immune to reflection
Beguiled into thinking it's for their protection
Placated by constant vapid confections
Which subtly act as appropriate deflections
Designed to distort truths true detection
Inevitably suppressing their own resurrection
Groomed to deny any cogent correction
Which would foster a new enlightened direction
Unshackling self-imposed constraints of suppression
From this constant denigration, a festering infection!

Methodically perpetuated by false nobilities
Historically perceived as purveyors of clarity
(But) Seldom tempering temerity with charity
Yet often lacking the appropriate humility
To adjudicate and rule with benign civility.
In order to garnish their own abilities

In gratitude supporting their noble utilities
Bereft of attitudes unleashing atrocities
Such as arrogance fueled with sick ferocity
Directed at any who'd oppose their hypocrisy
(Thus) exposing the veneer of their false democracy!

And in so doing destroying the image
Of their constant vapid ongoing scrimmage
Freeing many from their need for pilgrimage
No longer finding their freedom(s) diminished
And their own life's dreams left unfinished
All constraints now removed limiting the glory
A new realm established for mankind's evolving story!

Conceived & transmitted by Jeff Forman @ 4:50-6:30 pm on September 20th 2015. All Rights Reserved. Line 24 added 12:25 am on March 1st of 2019.

Directly inspired by (re)-viewing the film The Man In The Iron Mask (1976)

THE FATAL FLAW OF THOSE (PREDATORS) WHO PLACE THEMSELVES ABOVE THE LAW

Those (wo)men who place themselves recklessly above the law
By so doing arrogantly flaunt a most fatal flaw
The more they fan the flames of deception the more scrutiny they draw
As increased vigilance surely fells the most stubborn tree(s) like a crosscut saw!

When tyrants push the envelope of their unjust reign(s)
The people's wrath grows ever stronger in their justifiable disdain
In turn narcissistic paranoia grows within their confused brain(s)
Until it finally bursts like a wall obliterated by a wrecking balls crane!
The greater their attempts to broaden their dictatorial domain
The more complete the delusional grandeur ensures that they're insane!
And once that path is followed there's no way back in this cruel game
Because the routes may sometimes vary but the end result's (always) the same.
For every megalomaniac throughout history there's no renouncement or refrain
And eventually it all turns back upon itself destroying that from whence it came.
Have any wise men, saints or sages ever successfully sought to explain
The predatory seeds that elitists sow continually traversing this terrain?

For it seems that there's a common ground that they all unwittingly share

When they perpetually try to foist their dominant ways so lacking in care

And in so doing push the common folk to the limits of what they can bear

Until there's none that are still left that remain confused and unaware

Nor any that has not yet grasped that this enslavement's grossly unfair!

And through this devolution arise a select few who come to boldly dare

To deter and dethrone these purveyors of sacrilege who've renounced all prayer

With stout hearts and resonant minds they're ever vigilant ongoing sleuths

Who do not bend, break or turn from reason ever resolutely seeking truth

And despite all of the falsehoods thrown their way they glean the required proof

That dispels all of the twisted lies conspired by those unabashed and aloof

So that once again this seemingly undeterred Godless evil group

Is exposed embodying the tainted flaw and gene that defines this troupe!

Conceived & transmitted by Jeff Forman @ 9:30-10:50 pm on September 22nd 2015. All Rights Reserved.
Including minor revisions & tweaking late pm of December 4th & early am of December 5th 2015
Inspired/written after 18 minutes viewing of The Big Valley-#64 The Time After Midnight (Oct.2nd 1967).

THE QUEST TO RECLAIM THE REPUBLIC IN 2016 (INCLUDING THE IOWA CAUCUS JERK CIRCUS)

The latest round of politics
Has not been bereft of dirty tricks
Evidence abounds which one can trace
As always seems to be the case
No matter the faces or the places
This time Des Moine with wide open spaces.
The goal however remains the same
Despite how everyone plays the game
All players inevitably want to endure
So that they can be the one to procure
The ultimate victory and nomination
To usurp the crown of the Obamination
Who's brought our country to ruination
Increasingly fraught with cultural stagnation
He cares naught for our society's emancipation
Despite his story of increasing its glory
The result's been one of far more doing poorly!

Has there ever been a bigger phony?
Whose intent from day one was dispensing baloney!
The bigger his ego's vast inflation
The further his high self's degradation.
The more he destroys, the greater his elation!
The spectre of Obamacare ever sickening our nation
Continuing to implode with increasing putrification
Coerced with Nancy Pelosi's traitorous participation
Recklessly compounding her soul's increasing depreciation
Suffering the fallout via ever greater defamation

Would this nullify her initial projected false elation
Had she acted responsibly via introspective contemplation?
Might Hades also be her ultimate destination?
Certainly resultant adverse karma has been her creation!

Likewise Barrack's colossal gall will ensure his adverse downfall
His intentions to deceive will ultimately yield no reprieve
Rendering it more preposterous for anyone to believe
Much less even more farfetched for anyone awake to conceive
How his steadfast sycophants still cheer wildly in unison
The greater this megalomaniac's empty sad infusions
Like frothing zombies wild in their blissful delusion(s)
Reveling in their own orgies of collective confusion
How can we put a stop to their sacrilegious intrusions?
That further hastens our society's crumbling devolution!

Granted his handlers have been exceedingly shrewd
By installing a man who's far from a prude
Who continues brazenly thus far to elude
Any who choose to engage and bring feud
Perceiving (t)his character's both rude and crude
Not the cavalier braggart thinking he's such a (cool) dude
A really slick prick that now far surpasses
One called "Tricky Dick" who excelled in crassness!

No limits to the bureaucratic fudge he's dispensing
Spewing (out) egregious sludge (that's) further entrenching
Our people in crud encrusted with mud from this dud
As this wicked dope pummels our once fair Republic
Now reeling on the ropes, will it soon go up in smoke?
Never before assaulted with such dire a scope
Of foul gross depravity entrenched in insanity
A crazed megalomaniac increasing his power
The more he enslaves, the more he devours!

As many around him bow down and cower
Content to be underlings reaping the shower(s)
Of scraps he throws down from his high tower
Ultimately usurped by this (vain) arrogant twerp
Despite their malfeasance, their steadfast allegiance
Remaining fakes on the take in their predatory games
Rigged for their own sake from this snake increasing the stains
On their honor and souls from traitorous monetary gains
Like vapid trolls stoking the flames of control
With more noxious smoke as the common folk choke
And grow increasingly broke from the money they stole
Being raked over the coals as fuel for their own gruel!

It's a tale that's been told many times and it's old
Where the bold sold lies and suppress and withhold
Prosperity and truth, remaining coldly aloof
Fickle minions of evil intent to pervade
All civilizations and societies in which they evade
Both scrutiny and detection throughout most elections
Some point their fingers and others are ringers
Who don't peal out truths, rather render abuse
As they deal out fake falsehoods to steal and plunder
More wealth via stealth until finally they blunder
Polluting themselves with too much false thunder
No matter how many they trample asunder
Having crammed too much scam into their selfish plans
Not giving a damn in extending their flim-flam!

For awhile miring those less aware in a funk
Spewing out enough junk to choke a skunk
Until their engine of progress falters from gunk
A recent example was dispensed by Ted Cruz
So intent upon winning deciding to bruise
Ben Carson's campaign, tweeting he had quit

Which in fact was actually a load of shit!
And he knew it but saw fit to try and trick
Some of Carson's supporters to jump from his ship
In so choosing such a deceitful tactic
Albeit a less forceful form of press gang trick
Demonstrating a willingness to cheat and abuse
Rather than possibly yet nobly lose
It's also an apparent fact that Ted's in bed with Goldman Sachs!
Rest assured that anyone backing this fake joker
Will likely reap the shafts of their miscreant poker!

Their allegiances are strictly to their own ilk
What filth whose designs are to continue to bilk
The middle class as well as kick them in the ass
As well as the groin while they grope them for more coin
Via stealth enriching their coffers with more ill-gotten wealth!
Mattering naught for them possessing nary an idle thought
For those they're distressing, for they've been wholly bought
Not caring how much they steal nor how the poor people feel
Who pray to God as they kneel to feed their families their next meal!

The shredded veneer of our once proud democracy
All but rendered extinct from this putrid hypocrisy
Enacted by Democrats and Republicans alike
Who actually wear and share the same stripes
They might all as well have been on strike
In representing the American people
Many who have been their unwitting sheeple!

Falsely aligned divided against each other
Maintaining these traitors now dwindling cover
Who behind closed doors are one and the same
Continuing to orchestrate their evil games

Dispensing naught but gross deceptions
In each and every subsequent election
Almost since each parties inception!

Have we ever seen such a deviant collection?
That's awakened many who've arisen in convection
Creating a full-fledged spirited insurrection
Intent upon instilling an outright correction
So that they can facilitate a new direction
Via a healthy and helpful pure resurrection
So the false wealthy and stealthful receive just rejection!

They're now on the run trying to take our guns
Increasing the elitist shun as patriots (a)rise in unison
Soon their tyranny will fail and they'll end up in jail
As the uprising tsunami descends upon this scum
Like a tidal wave washing away these vile bums
Diffusing their arrogance like punctured hot air balloons
As they're catapulted asunder into self imposed gloom
Hurtling into the abyss that they'll be relegated to soon
Where they can forever ponder their earned abject doom!

As Justice Scalia's unusual demise results in many varying outcries
Will Obama's besmirched smirking face be obliterated with mace?
A narcissist's twisted legacy soon replaced with nary a trace?
Electing an administration no longer traitorous to our nation
A healthful transformation collectively embraced and put in place
Freedom and prosperity once again renewed restoring U.S. to grace
As We The People regain our power dethroning tyranny's false tower
Casting the Oligarchs down into the mud cowering in their own blood
Just as God's wrath purged the earth of rampant evil with The Flood!

From those on the left reveling in their own sea of prideful false glee
No limits to their vanity with immorality embraced but bereft of sanity
And those who are rightfully outraged yet saddened by such calamity
Their moral codes intact yet shaken awakened steadfast in humanity!

THE QUEST TO RECLAIM THE REPUBLIC IN 2016 PART TWO

Still Barrack's seemingly wasting no time in attempting to implement by false design
His latest vile stick a real liberal pick intending to inflict another radical shift
In the Supreme Court to further distort any justified legislation with more Obamination!
So that another chapter in this false clown prince's hollow laughter
Will forever be stained with his disdain which abounds with putrid renown
For a country built on freedom and truth that this foul stench of a man still brazenly aloof
Says yes we can change in more wretched false flag games the goal of which remains the same
To destroy all that was once held pure, no concern for what's sacred nor how long it's endured!

Seeding chaos and dissent fulfilling the psychotic intent of his handler George Soros who procured
More regime changing antics as a Nazi collaborator turned traitor leaving Jewish brethren frantic
As this ever satanic seed in dire mortal need continues to bleed rather than succeed and feed
A decrepit soul as an ongoing mole who blatantly stole their lives and their wealth through stealth
Feathering his blasphemous bed sowing instead increasing dread with ever more dead
As the looming spectre of Barry he's been grooming with great charity to distort more clarity
In people's perceptions, neither having limits in their rhetorical inflections imbued with deception!

What's sure to unfold is their tyrant's mold breaking forever ending their clever faking and taking

As the curtain's pulled back, this fast track to hell yielding no resurrection from such an infection

For any false followers fanning their flames of vanity with levels of depravity ensuring calamity

That can inevitably be traced back to these vile race baiters and haters, traitors to all of humanity

Sealed within the festering tombs that they've groomed for themselves of stark outright insanity

Causing many awakened justifiably outraged to lace their resulting condemnation with profanity.

Noble sages sidelined for ages once again restore the populous to reason freed again from treason

Birthing a new season delightfully grand to be-in dispatching all who've made their dates with fate

A blessing, as our society's convalescing after appropriate confessing rather than more distressing

As all patriots align in impressing a fortified benevolently slated state that's inherently great!

Rendering all tainted seeds of criminal families inbred destroyed instead forever unable to weather

The storms of their egregious making now no longer taking all Bushes and Clintons forever quaking!

Conceived & transmitted by Jeff Forman from 2:15 am-5:45 am on March 30th 2016. All Rights Reserved.
Initial first rough draft was written from 9:20 am-11:07 am on March 17th 2016.

THE QUEST TO RECLAIM THE REPUBLIC IN 2016 PART TWO CONTINUED

As Obama's assault on decency increases he's also hell bent inflicting relent-less evil without repent
Oblivious to the extent of growing resentment and dissent blinded fully despite this cowardly bully's
Legacies' fast crumbling in infamous tragedy as more hypocrisy's exposed by Judicial Watch's veracity
Who've doggedly chipped away the false veneer congress has complicitly held at bay unable to convey
Any truth, absent in their own duty and watch sidelined in stagnation treasonously deserting the nation
They swore to uphold and protect, resigned to full dereliction of duty cultivating lunacy with impunity
Soon to be corrected and disinfected with both dissected and divested of their own detestable invective
Unfurled for all to see and hurled into the dustbins of history as shameless failures infusing sad legacies
Of broken oaths to protect citizens who've now renounced them before they're trounced into oblivion!

If only they'd had a shred of humility and straightened their bowed backbones with renewed civility
Instead they continued their reckless paths unrenounced in restoring charity and prosperity with clarity
Of purpose, karmically sabotaging their tainted souls futures fainting away being tragic losers and users
No renewed vigor enabling their steeds remountable to uphold a balance of power and be accountable!

Conceived & transmitted by Jeff Forman from 2 am-3:45 am on April 2nd 2016. All Rights Reserved.
Initial first rough draft was written from 11:20 am-12:40 pm on March 17th 2016.

THE QUEST TO RECLAIM THE REPUBLIC IN 2016 PART THREE

For any folks truly aware it's quite unfathomable how Hillary's hubris can still possibly ensnare
Any backers when hackers have already breached untold security leaks because of this treasonous creep!
Yet quell all astonishment while resisting any admonishment giving no quarters for her rabid supporters
As any remaining must be insane having done no homework on this snide, conspiring, communist jerk!

Whose husband's rapeturous sexcapades assaulted the sanctity of many a maid leaving many quite staid
As well as stained with remorse that our thwarted justice system neglected to enforce, despite evidence
That anyone dense could plainly see was again blatant hypocrisy enabling a sexual predator to run free
To unleash further tyranny from a woeful Whitehouse entrenched in moral decay that surely reeks
Of rampant infamy enshrouded in the overwhelming stench of a failed democracy on display for weeks
Stretched into years of putridity while lingering stains of 911 are denied validity with ongoing hypocrisy!
It's no wonder to those clear that our country's been had by evil that's glad to destroy all once held dear!

As many live in fear that the Fed's retrieval from transgression will never yield to transparent confession

For it's grown into a monstrous infection that not only requires total suppression but evisceration, shown

By God's condemnation or inflicted in ire via nuclear strike to blacken the eye of a country sucked dry

By this vampire class that thinks the whole world should just kiss ass because they're not up to the task

Of dismantling their mass of total corruption intent upon rampant destruction unleashed with foul glee

Sans impunity, so soon a karmic backlash will be unleashed in kind with rampant fury of those aligned in

Hearts and stalwart souls too long confined by debauchery and treachery of all ruling classes who have

Renounced God and removed the moral glasses of the true nobility of their birthrights, squandered again

As the seeds of corruption and sands run out for these uncivil louts neglecting to invert their hourglasses

Perhaps no course left but outright revolt to remove and strike down these dolts via God's thunderbolts

The masses of all other classes combining disarming harmonies chiming in unison issuing the final jolts!

Conceived & transmitted by Jeff Forman from 4:45 am-6:55 am April 2nd 2016. All Rights Reserved.
Initial first rough draft was written from 5:20-5:22 pm & 5:25-6:53 pm on March 17th 2016.

THE CENTRAL PRANKS OF WORLDWIDE BANKS AND THEIR PARTNERS IN CRIME THE POLITICAL GRIME

We're living in a time of truly unprecedented crime
Our world being currently stuck with evil running amuck!
Confused governments recklessly use and savagely abuse
Their own people fleecing them like flocks of disposable sheeple!
Blatantly abusing their trust for their own greed and insane lust
For more wealth and power as they ravenously devour
Assets they can grab bending laws so that they can be had
As all central bankers worldwide conquer and divide
Their depositors in stealth increasing their own wealth.

Yet in secret some inside truthfully ruefully confide
To a select few behind closed doors to whom they implore
That they don't know what they're doing as they blow
Through more fiat printing yet their countries just keep sinking
Saddled with more debt which does nothing much less correct
The looming economic cliffs that they've created with their myths
Of rounds of quantitative easing wrongly thinking that they're pleasing
Their constituents in dissolving massive debt, rather than solving
These huge bubbles that are increasing everyone's growing troubles
As these tentacles are ever entangling like manacles further strangling
All economic growth so almost all countries are now dangling broke
Over cliffs of untold destruction that is largely due to their corruption!

Blinded by their own egos aligned with perceived false strategos
Like mad scientists crazed in collective confusion acting in total delusion!
Yet back in 2008 many fools thought they were really quite great
In staving off our collective fate saying they were simply too big to fail
When what should have entailed was most being derailed and put in jail!
But they're all still running free like inmates possessed with glee
Running amuck from their asylums thinking how clever they must be
So Wall Street runs unchecked screwing Main Street that they've wrecked
When really they're the bigger dopes who've yet escaped the looming ropes
That will soon descend upon their necks for they've utterly failed to mend
Their callous ways as they've ultimately been architects of their own last days.

Far fewer now can sing their praise despite them woefully getting a raise
Their money stained with the sweat and blood from those they've maimed
In the middle class now reeling from such ill gotten gains, so vile and crass
Has been the stew of their making that's boiling now like a witches brew!

Will this traitorous crew soon face mutiny as they come under further scrutiny?
For now the call's all hands on deck, their sinking ship will soon be wrecked

As it founders on the shoals, truly out of control because it was left unchecked
By politicians worldwide who abandoned morality, instead choosing to decide
To grant their co-conspirators a bye deceitfully accepting massive bribes
Rather than confiding and siding with the people, opting instead to divide
Adopting that old Communist play thinking wrongly they can keep them at bay
Not only to conquer them but further betray and enslave them en mass
In attempts to cement their ruling class now fomenting another impasse.

So once again they face massive revolt as the ire rises the backlash will jolt
All of them with such undercurrents of shock dispensed from their flocks
Nowhere to run nor hide from the tides overwhelming their ships, no safe docks
Remaining for these misfits who have feathered their nests with karmic distress
Such short-sighted bliss has gone amiss constricting their shallow success
With naught left for them to confess but they have wrought their own mess
Of lives now in freefall, chosen with freewill God grants equally to us all
Which they chose to abuse corrupted with power and greed that they used
To try and enslave with the evil games that these depraved again play
Will they never learn that such corruption only yields their own destruction?!

Angela Merkel seemingly shares allegiance to this corrupt recurring circle
And that of false oppressors be them invading molesters or other transgressors
As she attempts to punish all protesters who speak out against such treachery
Will such betrayal of her country and the German people who she's neglected
Ultimately result in outright revolt felling the false steeple she's now erected?
Her insight has since been jolted, overwhelmed with refugees since elected.

Likewise Francois Hollande's betrayed France with another socialist experiment
Disillusioning many falsely entranced bankrupting his regime with malcontents
Foolishly having faith in a flawed system revealed to be nothing but a prison
Of their own faking for those who gullibly foster belief in the illusion of taking
Rather than making their own prosperity yielding relief from a culture breaking!

In Greece the people also found that turmoil and unrest abound in servitude
Their future fleeced from bank bail-ins as these gangsters still immorally elude
The wheels of karmic justice content to be amongst those so recklessly (c)rude
In apparent disregard for morals content to largely rest on such false laurels
Reaped in seeming immunity from prosecution fomenting tumultuous quarrels!

The European stage has again been set to engage and enrage with much killing
As no sages can quell the tumultuous rage building that the elite craft as gilding
On the thorny crowns of deceit which they adopt and wear so brazenly chilling
Flames of unrest once again fanned by the central pranks of worldwide banks!!

Here in the U.S. we're not far behind, this chaos and madness grows and shines
On the horizon orchestrated by the tantamount failure of the ruling class misers
Whose policies have always been to divide, plunder and trash, none the wiser!
Will the wild card Donald Trump continue to pump up those very disillusioned?
Who unite aligning in unison to dump the quaking status quo's abject confusion
Prompting a growing tidal wave to swamp and stomp those ruthless evil factions
Diffusing throwing back their baseless truth-less attacks impeding their traction!
Will We The People unite to exorcise the criminal District Of Corruption faction
Which has invaded, pervaded and entrenched themselves intent on distraction
From within all levels of our government and media, Hell bent on destruction
Of everything dear and just that our founders crafted within The Constitution!

It's high time that all peoples unite throughout planet earth in steadfast union

Girding themselves in truthful clarity projecting love and light together in unison

With unlimited collective insight for right humanity will surely endure and cure

The ills of this festering tyranny of chaos and division vanquished into oblivion

Along with those perpetraitors who by design or default were its active minions!

Forever banished to the depths of the netherworlds that spawned their making

Unable to survive in the blinding light of truth that will leave them all quaking

Amongst all denominations of race or religion no longer demanding nor standing

Against humanity's progress with all remaining purely vested in commanding

That none will espouse dominance or surveillance of others with false branding

Rendering all now accountable for their words, deeds, and actions simply loving

Everyone as sisters and brothers with total respect and love for one another

So that everyone's worth every day from their birth is valued as by our creator!

Conceived & transmitted by Jeff Forman on March 6th/ 7th, 2016 @ 5 pm.- 2 am. ALL RIGHTS RESERVED.
Including substantial additions & revision to final segment from 2/24/16 beginning with Angela Merkel.

TRUTH OR TYRANNY

The history of mankind has been fraught with many conflicts
Thousands of years past saw times of battles fought with sticks
This century's just begun with another threat called ISIS.
Nomadic tribes roamed various lands which they sought to command
Skirmishes shifted as the sands of hourglasses misted
during many stands
Resulting in the spawning of more civilizations dawning,
yet none could withstand
Eventual pummeling of corrupt governments tumbling,
funneling prosperity!
Always lasting for awhile until posterity soon resulted in temerity
During less industrious times as some fasted with dwindling charity
Curing famine from those more illustrious
is not often within their clarity!
Instead most opted to increase those suffering
as a crass form of buffering
Them further away from the masses
who they viewed as lower classes once deemed castes
Believing they were far superior, deeming some less entitled inferiors
Blurring the edges of their reason
until they resorted to outright treason!
This soon meant they adopted tyranny producing many suffering outcries
Along with tears falling on deaf ears,
to those with eyes it should come as no surprise
The advent of these self destructive seasons
ensured their eventual demise!

Conceived & Transmitted by Jeff Forman from 12.30-1:45 pm on March 7th, 2016. ALL RIGHTS RESERVED
Typed & tweaked + 2nd last line added from 3:17-4:25 pm on October 12th, 2018. Title 12:27 am 3/27/14.

ANTICS OF EARTHS TREE DWELLING RATS

Not sure of the extent of actual stats
Compiled relaying well documented facts
Nor deemed through research as exact
Of records achieved still leaving them intact
But if you own any acreage or land tracts
Their friendly presence will do naught to detract
Except garnering your attention to distract
Endowed with their truly unique special crafts
Squirrels are amazing arboreal acrobats!

Conceived & transmitted by Jeff Forman on March 26th 2016 from 3:15-3:27 pm. ALL RIGHTS RESERVED.
Lines 5 & 6 were conceived & added on April 7th 2016 & line 7 was added/conceived on April 14th 2016.

A (LONG OVERDUE) CONFESSION FROM THE EGREGIOUS MESS CALLED CONGRESS

It gives me no pleasure I most regretfully confess
That I must call out as incompetent our current Congress
Few of whom seem to suffer any noticeable distress
Most utterly blind to their own devolved sickness!

Once standing proud with integrity firm and steadfast will of purpose unyielding
Bereft of backbone impoverished now with squeamish souls it has been fielding
If this was a professional sports team most of its constituents would be fired
Untainted blood's required to restore a sickly body that should be retired NOT rehired!

A new class of people needs to apply who are NOT prone to defy but rather comply
With The Bill Of Rights and The Constitution as an institution that duly applies
Itself with actions entrenched in decency and reason rather than immersed in outright treason
As its current festering condition serves to blatantly impress upon many it's an egregious mess!
Likewise the senate and the house are also largely languishing in anemic distress
Requiring serious fumigation to remove much choking stagnation of those repressed!

In Diane Feinstein to put it mildly we have an old relic whose reason has lost its shine

So quick to take issue with constitutional critics, now just a pandering senile cynic

Immune to any valid new thinking with a high self subdued that keeps on shrinking

No longer able to hurdle the confines of her own ego which is content to selfishly mimic

The mainstream pundits who can't escape their self imposed redundancies as lame critics

Content to grovel for more trappings in their gilded hovels filled with material abundance.

Has their sight for right become so dim within, so short on stature and substance

That they can no longer summon courage and resolve to solve issues with a steadfast stance?

It's readily clear that they're just cowering in fear deserved of all hurled derogatory jeers

As utter failures co-opted by their dark sides where almost all of their souls now reside

For few openly lament their current descent, so what can compel any to ruefully confide

When most are quite simply children to chide, immune to adult failures deserving deride.

Is it any wonder that the stench of their entrenchment is now yielding 91% resentment?

Isn't it even more jolting and disturbing that 9% haven't renounced their own contentment?

With an organization that's festering imbued with so much dysfunction that an injunction

Should be put forth by concerned citizens to relegate it to burial and permanent extinction

It has outlived its purpose to enact the will of the people now treated ONLY like sheeple!

So how much longer can such worthlessness be given a bye when most don't even try
To right their course with serious discourse that's acted upon by resolute resourceful souls
Resistant to external control by internal trolls and moles who've already bartered their souls
Few of whom can actually come clean much less redeem their own darkness for light
By rekindling their pilot lights awakening in fright on stray plight-filled paths so lacking insight
Most have gone too far astray with their moral compasses betrayed, too compromised to fight
For freedom and truth content to be benign with their crimes and aloof to mountains of proof
That they have failed miserably, some so egregiously that they should be jailed but not assailed.

Let's see, we have Nancy Pelosi whose Botox injected face can no longer serve to embrace
Any place or position that's not in gross opposition to any worthy legislative injections!
John Boehner had sense via recompense to resign in dismay rather than continue to convey
An anemic presence, replaced with another disgrace named Paul Ryan who isn't even tryin'
To restore stature to the GOP as speaker of the house, content to be another emasculated mouse!
Sucking up to more treasonous acts by a jackass who defames and defiles a once white house
Totally devoid of any acts of patriotism, instead maniacally intent upon a total derisive schism

Of our former society, with barely a whimper denouncing its own gross impropriety!

I am far from alone in being horrified and decry that the detestable District Of Corruption
Diseased from within from its core of international crime that requires total evisceration
With the universal conviction of awakened souls worldwide aligned in an outright eruption
Of cleansing that's tantamount to the great flood and evils final eviction and restriction!
Thus freeing ALL of humanity fully to live in peace and prosperity ongoing with endless depictions!

Initial rough draft was written from 10:30 am-2:13 pm on May 30th 2016. All Rights Reserved.
Conceived & transmitted with minor revisions by Jeff Forman from 3:05-5:15 pm on May 30th 2016.

FURTHER PROOF IN THE ABSENCE OF ALL TRUTH WHEN THE BRAZENLY ALOOF REFUTE THEIR CO-CONSPIRING, WITNESS THE RECENT CONTORTION OF THE MISCARRIAGE OF JUSTICE DEPT. DISTORTION REQUIRING AN ABORTION & RE-HIRING

As the daily debacle of the Obama administration wreaks havoc with its plethora of flagrant violations
I am compelled sans elation to be a voice for those seeking justice suffering great consternation!
As Judicial Watches' ongoing investigations along with others worthy of mention has led to aggravation
Fast and Furious rages on engaging many with its nest of co-conspirators maintaining spurious allegations!
The falsehood of this corrupt regime reigns supreme with a darkening sheen to its gleam of infestation
Pronounced in depravity like an abscessed cavity of pollution that's not an illusion with further intrusion
Of another disgraceful Attorney General despite a brief relief and mildly contrite Eric Holders' resignation
I solemnly rejected Loretta Lynch, an outright cinch to continue this eruption of corruption conflagration!

A perverse Obamination stoking a rotting empire with more refuse for the funeral pyre he's conspired
To destroy all vestiges of privilege that America once inspired with insatiable ire needing to be retired

From disservice of all people he wants to slaughter, this plotter against humanity ups his level of insanity
Which further abounds astounding all who see the fall of democracy he, his minions destroy with glee!

Witness the recent contortion, the miscarriage of Justice Departments distortion requiring an abortion
Thanks to Loretta Lynch truly being out to lunch, a profane dunce whose impropriety meeting Slick Willie
Can only be deemed contemptuous folly, not jolly happenstance for those not entranced by dame Hillary
Who's fully divested herself from any meager spiritual wealth and standing, brazenly aloof to being truthful
Yet seeking commanding the American people as president when as a former resident with Bill, youthful
They made a mockery of justice besmirching that former once white house darkening on the hill in D.C.

Such calamity, the Republic felled like a tree eviscerated by a succession of putrid administrative decrees
Littered with an abundant abuse of power yielding ample proof in the absence of truth from those aloof
Who actively refute any attempts to align and reform them to a former standard of morality and neutrality
Tempered by a rationale of checks and balances thus making allowances for a lack of civility or humility
Some must be condemned when failing to mend their ways having strayed too far from paths conveyed
By God and their high selves who've been shelved and betrayed, no longer feeling dismayed much less saved
For their souls have become so decimated and profligate at the expense of shame with wickedness and evil
Their audacity further fueling their hubris infested games for petty gains sans refrain much less retrieval!

May they serve as solemn lessons to all that the downfall of humanity may rest upon those who confess

Our sins amidst the din and multitude of distractions our current society has unleashed with a passion via

Many detractions from what's still held dear, for those of us clear to follow paths more naked and sacred

Purveying good will and prosperity to all, instead of joining the ball, blindly and selfishly enriching downfall

Immune to reflection only increasing convection as the dizzying flames Satan embroils with entrapments

Succumbs many to join (t)his detachment, bereft now of reason to invoke a high priestess of treason for

Election, U.S. Americans, Brits who voted for Brexit much to their credit and all other nations worldwide

Must strive for a new realigned direction, unified as one race of humanity restoring sanity, resisting calamity

Renouncing and denouncing all of the Globalists, New World Order, United Nations conveyers and betrayers

Who are amongst those who have turned away from both freedom and truth, whether by design or default

Aloof in their abuse cowering within their guise of power seeking falsely to empower their own gestalt

Trapped in a vault of their own deception unwittingly instilling a correction and their evisceral convection

Resulting in a shower of blessings raining down from the heavens nurturing those who resisted infection

Who weren't so haughty to become flagrantly naughty, thus still apt for confession and thus resurrection!

Conceived & transmitted by Jeff Forman from @1:20 am-7:10 am on July 3rd 2016 All Right Reserved.
Title conceived and First Rough Draft and written on July 2nd 2016 from 1:30 pm to 5:30 pm.

WILL THE DEPARTMENT OF JUSTICE DISGRACE ERASE ITS OWN FORMER LUSTRE OR WILL IT SUCK IT UP AND MUSTER MORE BLUSTER TO AVOID INFAMY BY ARRAINING TYRANNY RESTORING CLARITY WITH RIGHTIOUSNESS AND REASON USHERING IN A BRAND NEW EDEN

For Loretta Lynch it's a cinch she's nothing but a plant who
apparently can't properly enforce her job
Making all patriots and many others want to sob
due to the D.O.J. being naught but a knob
of the Clinton's hobnob who continue to rob
not only their own brothers and sisters like festering blisters
But her own future karma as well,
does she also turn a blind eye to busting Big Pharma and hell?
You'd best wake up woman before it's too late
and you've sealed your own fate assuring a date with
Your petty hate making many irate, excepting Satan I postulate
who's got you marked down on his slate
for a future date you won't escape, and he's content to wait a little
longer which you'd better ponder!
For if you procrastinate much longer his lure will get stronger,
and then he'll reel you in for your sins of omission,

Because that's his mission for all commissioned that fail to jail
as their trust's gone bust entails that moves like a snail,
You'd best avail your position as time's running short so you'd best report
and do your duty to serve your country rather than be a flunky
for Barrack's harassment, Hillary and money!
'Cause right now you're a junkie awaiting your next fix
from his bag of dirty tricks, for as he pricks harder
Your future spiritual larder will be depleted along with karmic pluses deleted at your high self's expense!
Can you afford to fence more before you've been shown the door?!
I fervently implore you reconsider your options,
before this concoction you're mixing becomes so constricting
they'll be no future elixir for escape and you'll be just another rape
of the Clinton's corrupt machine!
For their own souls' futures are in such a depleted condition there's no hope of remission as they're already assured of perdition!
If the D.O.J. was still sound it would act very soon
as copious proof abounds it could then attain renown like a crown,
instead of remaining aloof despite mountains of condemning truth
continuing to astound, planting more frowns on nobility's face.
For proper paths can't be retraced if some fail to erase
gross transgressions flaunted boldly in place,
Immune to confession thus confounding their own resurrection
Like a growing infection omitting forthright detection,
are they so dense there's no cause for reflection?
Vapid trolls seeking re-election, thus fomenting an insurrection
unwittingly adding to Satan's collection
of miscreant souls as he whittles more poles
to mount their arrogant heads when they're stone dead!
When it's all done they'll have nowhere to run and it won't be fun
that they tried in vain to steal the guns!
Wrath and disdain's rapidly growing, these oppressors' cracks now showing through from them not towing the mark,

their future's stark growing ever more dark
as the tides are turning the seas of wrath churning!
They've failed in their urgings when they should have been yearning
for more wisdom and learning
To serve greater humanity and the planet
rather than provoke profanity and further stoke insanity
Thus fomenting potential calamity for us all,
we must call them out they've completely dropped the ball!
God's children are rising with many confiding rather than dividing;
Their might will be sure and swift as the New Worlds Order's boats
are already adrift
And the rising tides and people's army
Will lift up God's hand across all the earth's lands
Catapulting all transgressors off proverbial cliffs into the abyss
Where their moribund souls will eternally miss
any hope of regaining bliss because they were remiss!
The kiss of death within their midst, opting to dismiss
themselves from reason with self imposed treason.
Sadly they won't be part of the new season
where all survivors will delight in each other instead of fight
And try to smother the undaunted quest of greater humanity
embracing edicts and acts of sanity
Restoring any entranced to proper insight enhanced,
thus free to delight in their collective right might
To create a brand new Garden of Eden
with free will and pure hearts intact which all elect to be in!

First Rough Draft transmitted on August 15th 2016 from 11:09 am-12:13 pm & 12:42 pm-1:30 pm.
Revised & augmented by Jeff Forman from @2:15-6:23 am on August 16th 2016 All Rights Reserved.

WHY OH WHY DO WE HAVE AN FBI WHOSE FUNCTIONAL IMPOTENCE MAKES US WANT TO CRY FOUL??

Why do we have an FBI whose leader can't credibly tell us why
he won't even try to indict
The epic organized crime of the Clinton Foundation's flagrant
design serially oozing with slime
Jeopardizing national security with colossal impunity
of countless payoffs and untold bribes
Compounded with astounding internationally hacked email trails
literally miles wide
Some whistle blowers sadly confide
befuddling even the most astute esteemed scribes
Making us commoners of purer hearts and souls cry
as James Comey gives Hillary a complete bye
Was he just another unwitting participant
in a long line of victimized compromised buys?
His smug disgraced face should be replaced
having woefully given the entire FBI a huge black eye!
Forever compromised making our whole nation
heave a collective sigh, has their rule of law died?

As FBI director doesn't that render him a head inspector
designed to be an official corrector
A proverbial pillar of justice and democracy,
yet his hypocrisy's branded him an outright defector
Derelict in his duties relegating Hillary to impunity,
such lunacy steeped in corruption like Loretta Lynch,

Both nothing but outright wimps and willing pimps
in Hillary's corrupt systemic vendetta!
Physically a man of huge stature,
effectively belittling himself
historically to only hollow laughter
Proving he's a midget of a man far from robust
in conveying the public's trust, has he no shame?
Besmirching his name he should resign from the game
for any fame he had has now become lame!
Did Hillary once again prove she's got more gall
ironically directing yet another's fall from truth
Who remains aloof from throwing her on the pillory
still conquering civility devoid of humility?
If any were threatened by Hillary's fixers,
it's time for public confessions infusing defensive elixirs
He's effectively defected to save his craven life steeped in strife
his high self pierced with a knife!

Mr. Comey's chosen profession in life like others before him can
be seen much like a balloon
As a seed sown it's grown via nurtured application
it receives inflation like a billowing mushroom
Supported by a robust stem rising higher
it propagates itself further and farther dispensing spores
Like an explorer leaving a trail that can be followed
even when agitated its essence still hallowed.
No matter the type of fungi or spore it continues to explore
its own destiny within nature's store
Wielding its vitality steeped in its own neutrality of purpose
immune to confusion or disillusion
It's being forever free to be teeming,
never held back nor compromised by plotting or scheming
Ultimately maintaining the sheen of an unfettered life's purpose
wondrously radiantly gleaming!

Some folk's careers that don't become tainted
follow similar paths of growth and enhancement
Resisting any self-nullification realizing its naught
but self-deprivation through false entrancement
For this will tarnish their value thus breeding
a more sallow seeding and reading of their life's scroll
An undercurrent duly self-imposed by design or default
it matters not some might say who enroll
For in final reckoning it's just another day
perhaps filled with dismay for those of us weakened
With abject conscience contrite nonetheless if we truly confess
our sins amidst the din and dings
Of life ringing upon us often creating strife,
yet that's the ongoing fight within and plight of being!
A consistent persistent test of character we all share,
sometimes becoming ensnared yet seeing
circumstances differently, some reacting sufficiently
with stout resolve able to extricate and absolve
their selves from the foibles encountered efficiently,
Whereas others less able resistance dissolves
Given enough external pressure
to erode internal measures of defense against their core beliefs,
Perhaps through grief or their own conceit
some sink so low to excuse themselves being cheats
Relegated to becoming freaks of nature,
consciences set aside rendering their own futures bleak!

Our 21st century's rife with copious strife,
as the odious spite of false purveyors of power cower
Behind their veneer of glamour to pummel and beguile us all
with their apparent might that's sour!
Specifically embodying these horrific traits both crudely and lewdly
are Hillary and Bill Clinton

Whose colossal gall continues to enthrall some and appall many,
as their infamy grooms conditions loom
like a festering cancer increasing the rancor
they're infusing with their abusive emissions!

A wise sage might contrarily see them
as valuable personages on display, along with other knaves named
Obama, Holder, Koskinen, Lynch, McConnell, Pelosi and Ryan,
who all betray our fair U.S.A.
For by design or default they have incarnated to highlight
how the unchaste can selfishly abuse might,
Lending insight into ultimate paths of salvation
for mankind's collective amalgamation
In its quest seeking eventual emancipation,
so all can avoid and avert its potential looming downfall
If righteousness isn't heeded by the appropriate wisdom needed
as future history books recall.
Thus conveying that mankind ultimately succeeded
when it was properly and virtuously seeded!

The question remains can these current rogues regain their reason
thus regretfully and effectively
Altering their own courses with infusions of required shame
to avert their abject treasonous ways!
Can they summon such levels of resolve to dissolve
the darkness holding their souls captive one day?
Reversing their division of the human race
in order to hold any more gross transgressions at bay
Electing instead the appropriately needed confessions
to ensure resurrection of their souls again!

As many resolute servants contrarily rise up in unison
more of humanity awakens to support truth and the light,
As insight's rising in crescendo, darkness retreats,
its innuendo's fading showing proof
That soon it'll be relegated to bygone annals of human history,
as its wiser ongoing collective path again evades its own extinction
pulled back from the brink of deception with sagely detection
Rendering needed convection for its balloon to inflate
rising up farther above a lovely landscape
Of beloved planet earth being the place of our birth
supporting our collective harmonious worth!

Title and verse 1 rough draft conceived & transmitted on November 10th, 2016 from 10:49-11:10 am

Verse 2 rough draft conceived & transmitted by Jeff Forman on December 9th, 2016 from 12:33-1:16 pm

Verses 3-8 rough drafts conceived & transmitted by Jeff Forman on December 9th, 2016 @1:40-3:53 pm

Substantial editing, additions & revision to format online from @10:45 pm-6:30 am December 10th, 2016

THE PATHOLOGY OF MEGALOMANIACS WHO'VE STRAYED FROM TRUTH

All megalomaniacs disdain truth, lacking insight
cultivating fright with pathologic delight
In their flight from the light, as darkness pursues them
enthused madness fuels their cruel fear!
Less clear, it invades their souls as shades of grey
pervade their essence, no longer able to extol virtue
Their sense of reason denied now publicly decried,
their moles and trolls also deprived as inept spies
Left in the lurch, by those more alert to pave the way
for better days to come for some to savor
Rather than opting to betray their fellow men, who yen
for ascension renouncing dissension and division
In their just missions never aloof, in proof
maintaining their youth as soothsayers and conveyers of truth!
Never betrayers acting in stealth compounding false wealth
thus destroying their own spiritual health!

Conceived & Transmitted by Jeff Forman from 3:30-4 am on December 23rd, 2016 ALL
RIGHTS RESERVED
Typed and Tweaked with minor additions and revisions from 5:25 pm-5:50 pm on
October 12th, 2018

POWER PROMOTES
PROSPERITY WITH CHARITY?

Our power promotes Your prosperity!
We say that with our full sincerity
Despite there being a greater disparity
We (can) assure you of better future clarity
Increasing our coffers ensures greater charity!

By procuring more capitol with increasing alacrity
We're confident you'll (soon) find conditions quite satisfactory.
That will further insure against any impending calamity
Or a societal backlash of justifiable profanity.
None of us desires any acts or outbreaks of insanity
Remember Our collective power promotes All of humanity
And rest assured you can bet that that's not just serving our vanity!

Speaking of which we'd be remiss if we don't fully dismiss
Any doubts that people want to vociferously shout out.

Because in advance we need to keep you suitably entranced
Your lives can't help but be enhanced (by) being increasingly well financed
And the distance between us decreased with such a new found alliance
Remedying any ills with full societal digital compliance!
And rest assured that any potential dissenters who rise in defiance
We'll crush in a relentless rush to nullify any and all would be tyrants
Who might just filter in with the giant insurgence of all justifiable migrants
Many of whom will certainly serve as additional democratic clients!

Conceived and transmitted by Jeff Forman from 2:20-3:00 pm on June 22nd, 2017
Typed & tweaked with first editing + the addition of line #5 on June 25th, 2017 from
4-5:00 pm.
Further revision from 6:40-8:00 pm on July 9th, 2017 with last line added. ALL RIGHTS
RESERVED.

THE VALUE OF HONOR, A PRICELESS GIFT NOT TO BE BARTERED OR SQUANDERED

The value of honor is timeless and priceless
To not be a goner one must be entice-less
Can we all evolve to become truly vice-less?
And profoundly renounce all acts of divisiveness!
Is that not the true test of one's ultimate success?!
In order to be the best in each lifetime's eternal quest
We must all divest ourselves from urges of pettiness
And resist our ego's penchants for chest thumping shallowness
Instead maintain our high-self's vested interests like crests
Of steadfast valor honoring those who best act to serve the rest
For can we truly then honor ourselves with anything less?!
When we lay our bodies down again to rest without any distress
Left for our souls to ponder nevertheless much less to confess,
That our life's journeys may have strayed from our hearts guidance within our chests
Yet our somewhat tattered vests have still withstood the tests
That life's roads travelled have bestowed upon us with enrichness
The wisdom to grow like grand gardens flourishing in the wilderness!
Those most profoundly beautiful duly recognized and universally blessed!

Transmitted & conceived by Jeff Forman @ 8:50-9:42 pm on September 23rd, 2017. All Rights Reserved.

Written in free flow without need for editing & immediately inspired while re-watching for the 2nd time The 3rd Pirates of the Caribbean film "At World's End "paused at @1:04:45 where Geoffrey Rush playing Captain Barbossa says "Shame they're not bound to honour the code of the Brethren isn't it? Because honour's a hard thing to come by nowadays", to which Chow Yun-Fats character replies "There is no honour to remaining with the losing side. Leaving it for the winning side that's just good business!

Additional underlying influence and inspiration came from Esperanza: Excerpt from Mother by Maxim Gorky, a copy of which hangs on the wall adjacent to my Baldwin grand piano.

Typed & minimally tweaked with last line added @4:20-4:21 am on September 24th, 2017.

ESPERANZA

There will come a time, I know,
When people will take delight in one another,
When each will be a star to the other,
and when each will listen to his fellow as to music.
The free men will walk upon the earth,
men great in their freedom.
They will walk with open hearts,
and the heart of each will be pure of envy and greed,
and therefore all mankind will be without malice,
and there will be nothing to divorce the heart from reason.
Then life will be of one great service to man!
His figure will be raised to lofty heights—
for to free men all heights are attainable.
Then we shall live in truth and freedom and in beauty,
and those will be accounted the best who will
the more widely embrace the world with their hearts,
and whose love of it will be the profoundest;
those will be the best who will be the freest;
for in them is the greatest beauty.
Then will life be great,
and the people will be great who live that life.

Excerpt from MOTHER by Maxim Gorky

THE TRANSFORMATION OF MEGALOMANIACS BACK FROM MADNESS TO HEARTFELT GLADNESS!

As with all megalomaniacs, psychopaths and sociopaths
who wrongly stray down evil pathways
They revel in their own depravities foisting it upon others
they should sincerely revere as brothers.
Yet instead they smother in the festering cavities of their brains,
once sane before their moral fibers became rewired,
Now mired in ire that could only be sired by a demonic presence
defiling their essence
Which was once pure, but must have been forced to endure
some serious trauma with such an event
That it sent them to a dark place which they've since embraced,
still bereft of an appropriate cure to lure
Them back to the light with proper insight
dispelling their earlier fright in their flight from enlightenment
At their own souls expense, now facing truth
with its inherent recompense restoring their common sense!
Redeeming its former wealth no longer being embalmed in stealth
but again becoming purely heartfelt!

Conceived & transmitted by Jeff Forman @7:42-7:52 pm January 3rd, & 6:28-6:35 pm January 8th, 2018
Titled 10/11/18. Typed w' minor revisions @6:45-7:25 pm on October 12th, 2018 ALL RIGHTS RESERVED.

GLORIFYING THE UNIFYING POWER OF SHOWERING PEOPLE'S LIVES WITH PURPOSEFUL TRUTH

Evil feeds upon the depravity of some people's goals that have
strayed from paths of purposeful truth yielding righteousness!
Creating cavities within their souls like burrowing moles
who play in earth's tunnels aloof to the light.

Wielding insight which overcomes fright thus nullifying flight,
aligning with wisdom as proof
that one's youth can be stained with the perils of fame
during life's recurring, tempestuous games
which strain against the chains of morality
that hold us to a more charitable, profitable reality!

Not succumbing to cowardly superficiality nor banality,
Sullying ill gotten gain renounced with disdain
by the quality of others being smothered
Thus denying one's sisters and brothers as inherently gifters!
Acting instead as drifters and gypsters,
covered by defections and deceptions
with misplaced bets short circuiting successes
and thus the higher resonance
of a well grounded, magnanimous presence!

Not diluting one's essence by pollution and recklessness,
Opting instead for infusions of service towards a higher purpose!
Not festering in mired foibles of fecklessness,
much less cowering or souring devoid of blessedness.

Instead nurturing, flourishing and flowering
allowing humanity to collectively resonate in harmony!
Disarming calamity and profanity with profound sanctity
restoring glorifying sanity!

Conceived and transmitted by Jeff Forman from 1:07 am-2:30 am April 12th, 2018 ALL RIGHTS RESERVED.
Typed & tweaked with minor editing on June 7th, 2018 from 6:24 am-7:25 am. Title conceived at 7:35am.
Further revised, typed & reformatted anew on August 20th, 2019 between 11:45 am to 1:25 pm.

THE SELF BETRAYAL AND DEMISE OF MAINSTREAM FAKE NEWS MEDIA PROMULGATED VIA STEALTH USURPED BY THE REASON AND GENESIS OF A UNIFIED GREATER HUMANITIY'S COLLECTIVE WEALTH

Has it ever been more increasingly apparent with copious evidence mounting and abounding?

That our mainstream media's willingly anti diffident, laced with notorious petulance astounding

In its lame-stream assault on the truth, chillingly non-repentant in its continuous abuse

Admonishing our duly elected president Donald Trump, whose actions being meritorious in use

Confounding the Deep State's efforts to campaign with distraction a constant capriciously obtuse misuse,

Resounding in a cacophony maligned with fatal infection resultant in malicious confuse

Compounding many less clear now aligned with mortal defection repugnant in some vicious youth aloof

Co-opted by slander, their reason now meanders in ruin swept like a broom into a withering room

That's naught but a tomb, dooming any illustrious futures in attempts hijacking those more industrious

In tune and immune to distortion that's a contortion of reality, potentially diluting any inherent regality

Which our unified humanity can signify if it collectively defies this insurrection fed by depravity,

A cavity of fake news pendants, redundant in feeding their fallacious facades of false countenances
Imbued with their rude repugnance, pronounced in their chillingly stark, gross announcements
Defying reality in their collective bestiality like a pack of ravenous dogs that must be flogged into submission,
Their rabies put down renounced with attrition unconditionally defied and unclogged
Deprogramming their phony transmission(s) as missionaries of mercy to those less worthy
Suffering from the scurvy of their fallout, left turns who've dropped out of step with the rest who've not lost their beat
To dethrone the elite, realizing collectively that we can surely more than compete in unison
But diffuse all confusion and illusion, trumping dissolution and dilution of clearer, collective perception
Yielding appropriate detection infusing a resurrection fueled by convection, no disconnected defections
Kick-starting the Genesis of genetic correction of greater humanity's synergistic connection!

Conceived and transmitted by Jeff Forman from 6:12 pm-7:44 pm on April 22nd, 2018
Title by 7:52 am
Typed and tweaked with minor revisions from 6:00 am-7:07 am, May 19th, 2018 ALL RIGHTS RESERVED

DECEPTION DENOUNCED AND RENOUNCED, PERCEPTION ANNOUNCED AND PRONOUNCED!

Have you succumbed to the vile deception?
It's a massive infection by an evil insurrection
Led by a Deep State run by fallen souls consumed with hate!
Massively irate who've sealed their own fate assuring a future date
In Satan's lair, always gleeful for more inmates,
those irretrievably impaired,
Who've recklessly renounced their own care,
wallowing in despair; What, no recourse in Godly prayer?
As they're denouncing spreading truths
spewing many ongoing spoofs, flagrantly aloof
From accountability, their growing instability
infused with pathologic culpability
Denying all civility for decades, as has Hillary,
her pillory prepared from venomous shillery!
The perfect, political prostitute
conjoined to the prostitute fake news media,
Encyclopedias of rejected ethical attributes,
aligned with institutes of half baked academias
Staffed with defected, immoral, sterile goofs
confined to groups these graft staked deceivias!
The question to ask as they bask
in their spurious fake banter canter,
Are they masks of infection unto themselves
ensconced within broken planters soon to be taken to task?
By those who seek the light willing to fight for what's right,
nonetheless contrite with no delight
For their fallen brothers and sisters
who have been blistered into outlandish resisters!

112

Their usurped, impaired reason infused with such virulent treason,
deserving of much greivin'
Tempering much resultant seethin'
we God serving patriots hold for all heathens!
Our collective is steadfast and strong,
prolonged in tradition an ongoing, justifiable mission!
No invectives will last enabling attrition,
only those growing Godly adorable commissions
Those of us denounced as deplorable will collectively rejoice,
ever glowing in eminent decisions!

Conceived & transmitted by Jeff Forman from 1:48-4:34 am on May 17th, 2018 ALL
RIGHTS RESERVED
Typed and tweaked with minor editing and revisions from 4:30 am-5:44 am on May
19th, 2018

FROM ELOQUENCE TO RELEVANCE AS FALSE HYPOCRISY FULFILLS DEMOCRACY

Without spouting fluff some of us used to believe in a man
who spoke eloquently named Trey Gowdy.
Much doubting stuff abused he conceived of the clan
who faked relevancy once famed but now dowdy.
Such pouting gruff enthused we believed wouldn't stand
as baked decency contained, yet still rowdy!
Shouting bluff confused, naught achieved, couldn't fan
snuffed, staked complacency stained, shilling loudly!
Confounding enough misused sought bereaved, shouldn't brand
mistaked malignancy feigned, killing proudly?
Astounding less tough diffused bought reprieved, didn't command
unbraked hypocrisy deemed willing provocatively.
Admonishing pests infused thoughtlessly naïve, can't commend
tamed bureaucracy gleaned, mitigating autocracy!
Astonishing despots' neutered effectively, deleted miscreants attend
shamed aristocracy cleaned, instilling fulfilling democracy!

Conceived and transmitted by Jeff Forman from 7:00 pm-8:30 pm w'title @ 8:35 pm
on June 6th, 2018
Typed on June 7th, 2018 4:34 am to 5:04 am. ALL RIGHTS RESERVED

THE LINES ARE DRAWN SINCE EVIL WAS SPAWNED, BY SPEAKING YOUR VOICE ARE YOU PART OF THE DECEPTION, OR WILL YOU BE PART OF THE DEFECTION TO ENABLE THE APPROPRIATE CORRECTION?

When it comes to a proper dissection of the countries past election,
a fair majority chose a correction
Due to the direction the country was sliding,
perceived as a massive defection away from the perfection
Which the constitution outlined as a solution
to tyranny's attempts to subjugate humanity as a dilution
of freedom that our forefathers deemed devolution via absolution,
creating a schism, a justifiable mission
Instilling certain conditions, tilling new ground
absolving grievous killing, those devious guilty of unsound commissions!
Such long standing attrition without permission to be abated
was no longer tolerated, they migrated to be satiated.
No longer fated to endure, thus remedying a cure to ensure
life free from strife!
Defying trying conniving which yielded more dying,
sighing can now be erased and replaced with thriving!

Conceived & transmitted by Jeff Forman from 7:14-8:45 am, July 16th, 2018. Title
8:57/9:03 pm 7/15/18.
Typed & Tweaked with minor editing from 7:40-10:00 pm, Sept. 30th, 2018. ALL RIGHTS
RESERVED.

THE FALSE HYPOCRISY OF SOME FEIGNED ARISTOCRACY TEMPERED BY TIME MEDIATING NO CRIME CONFUSED WITH FALSE GUILT INFUSED, DIFFUSED BY ONE SO SUBLIME SO ANGELIC SHE SHINES!

Sometimes the crimes most grievous in one's life
are those creating inner strife
Suppressing regrets to uphold (the) status quo
does naught for confessing internal woes!
This inner foe must be quelled by freeing feelings self compelled,
both shelved and withheld
At the expense of maintaining a defense upholding false pretense
that's grown truly immense!
Weighing down one's free will like choking upon a bitter pill
countermanding life's quest to fulfill
The thrill of love instilled from angelic infusions above,
like doves diffusing all confusion and illusions!
Dissolving false fences no matter how deeply entrenched,
spirit doth freed to now recommence
Its purposeful path with reclaimed staff in hand,
ready to redeem any dreams it commands!
All harmful wrath ballooned, consumed and passed like sand
traversing the hourglass, cast to the winds
Like self imposed sins creating such internal dins within
throughout our lives like hives!
Which we've allowed to grow and even sow as blows
to our livelihood, no longer fostered, freed now and understood!

Forgiving ourselves and all as we should, knowing
we could now open our hearts to full expansion sublime!
No longer allowing depreciating thoughts to confine
the true expression we all have to angelically shine!
Radiantly bathing and enthralling in the glares
of wondrous gifts we uniquely share all pristinely defined!

Re-watching Rebecca (1940) was the direct inspiration for writing this poem on 9/16/18 after the film.
Joan Fontaine represents the angel in my title who saves & redeems the character of Maxim de Winter played by Sir Lawrence Olivier from himself & his personal demons with the purity & sanctity of her love.

Conceived & Transmitted by Jeff Forman @ 5:35-8:12 pm, Sept. 16th, 2018. Titled 3:16/4:16 pm 9/16/18.
Typed and tweaked with minor editing from 2:04-3:00 pm October 1st, 2018. ALL RIGHTS RESERVED.

ALL RENOUNCED WRONGS
TRANSFORMED WITH SONG!

A slack jawed grin sure ain't no sin when displayed for ones kin
amidst a din when it could wear thin
During a feud, whether pie-eyed or stewed
from a moonshine just brewed, or lewd inference crude
Made in jest or in song as they all sing along in a unified throng
which could all go quite wrong
From an ill advised thong, compromised by a prong
from an avid Don Juan whose dong just became a mite long!
This irrepressible zeal which he couldn't conceal,
much less suppress when put to the test by a lusty lass
Whose proverbial sass sure wasn't some crass ass,
nor a fated impasse pouted towards a fresh lout
Who's veined member thrust out, leaving no doubt
the most dim-witted cringing it was ready to spout
From an over amped vamp's alluring pout,
unleashed with an unbridled shout from her foul mouth!
In such sexual glee it was really something to see for free,
or even a modest fee if deemed necessary,
Surely not for quaint folk despite prior vows bespoke,
who've been cowed like two beasts bonded in yoke
Tamed in tandem not random by a contained society
over endowed with propriety, to nip notoriety one must promote piety,
Maintaining proper decorum as adjudicated via forum
by an adequate quorum ample scorn applied for 'um!
But times have changed with past mores rearranged,
no longer detained nor arraigned with false stain
Played by those profane applied by their own shame
in a game claimed as just,
Tempering those more natural tendencies to apply thrust
with a mite more unbridled lust!

Freeing those crustier to be just a trifle lustier,
crop dusting more spores to alleviate confining mores!
Transforming some formerly depressed and deplorable
into much healthier, warmer, affectionate, adorable!
Freed from false shackles to cackle in unison,
Holy Mackerel such crooning can become quite consuming
In soothing former unadorned fuming,
like smoke pluming free for now all can see
Such confining ropes were only for dopes
who'd eloped with false dins of proverbial sins, now worn thin!
To cast out like louts in disguise, that clouded some eyes
cleared to gaze upon skies, freed from all lies!
Aligned with unbounded love dispensed from above, archangels
sing, heavens ring in glorious song, reveling in humanity's throng!

Conceived & Transmitted by Jeff Forman @6:53-8:51 am 9/30/18 & typed 10:26 pm-12:20 am 10/1/18 ALL RIGHTS RESERVED

SELF JUDGEMENT DULY INFLICTED FROM CHILDHOOD EMOTIONS BEING CONFLICTED TO WHICH ONE UNRULY CRUELLY SUCCOMBED WITH ANOTHER SADLY FALSELY CONVICTED

During lifetimes that humans endure and experience
oft' times clear seeing is veiled cured with pretence.
How can one aptly condemn rash actions taken
under extreme duress as actually being cruelly mistaken
When deemed sin from crass events yielding insufferable reactions
taken in impasse long to be forsaken?!
How can children be condemned much less amended
when conflicted with pains of cruelty conveyed,
Lashing out in rage to diffuse the outrage unfairly inflicted,
being confused with abuse not restricted,
When it appears that violent emotions
are sometimes the sole antidote to such virulent commotions?!

If only the promotion of clearer perceptions
would have tempered the convection of such an infection
In hindsight with momentary mediating reflection
being instilled as an immediate cleansing correction!
A simple redirection of confused ire quelling the fire
of those justifiably inflamed in the interactive game of life,
Where strife often comes calling
at most inappropriate times galling, even the sanest then falling
Into its trap with a gap in reason, its treason
can befall any and all when we're oh so small and in season!

Ripe for malfeasance weakened in credence
temporarily unable to forestall, a storm of emotions within
Which we must meet head on before they spin
us rashly away from clarity, steeped in the stark severity
Of false temerity which we must resist with charity
extended to ourselves and others, being our brothers
And sisters who in trying times become flustered,
confused with shame and disdain for one another
Entrapped in the eddies of life's game,
where sometimes those vain can be consumed with false fame!
Content to claim the trappings that only become wrappings,
unable to mask those internal saplings
Which become sullied with sorrow, if and when borrowed
from truth during the vulnerability of youth!

May God provide proof, to keep them pure enough to endure
the trials enabled to procure providence
With resolute confidence not to invest in wiles,
nor engage in compliance with any weakened others
Who've cowered and covered their own internal sages
inappropriately disowned, who they must trust
Not to be smothered, instead recovered rendering self understood
when falling prey to false livelihood!
Never shamed, rather regained thus re-gamed
with life's best antidote for strife given, aptly enlightened
By unbounded gratitude and reason,
when augmented with heartfelt compassion it's always in season!

Conceived and transmitted by Jeff Forman from 10:15 am-12:38 pm on October 6th, 2018.
Typed & edited with minor revisions from 11:02 pm- 1:45 am October 7th, 2018. ALL RIGHTS RESERVED.

Directly inspired from watching the film The Strange Love of Martha Ivers (1946) on October 5th, 2018.
I resisted the strong urge to craft this poem until the following day knowing I would still be well guided!

This Oscar nominated drama featured superb performances by the interaction of its 3 stars (Barbara Stanwick, Kirk Douglas & Van Heflin very ably supported with his other potential female love quest /soul mate & savior played by Lizabeth Scott) whose lives were so provocatively depicted as to elicit the words I was guided by The Divine/The Universe/God to assemble here with my first draft. That took some time to type & tweak with minimal revisions & additions so as to configure the original content within the confining & demanding but always rewarding Microsoft Office Word 2007 online format!

THE FEDERAL BUREAU OF INSANITY HAS TRULY BECOME A VICIOUS CALAMITY (JUSTIFIABLY) OUTRAGING A SANE GROUP OF HUMANITY GIVING JUST CAUSE TO HURL SOME PROFANITY

This putrid corruption that's recently become a long overdue curtailed misguided eruption,
Stars some truly unruly, half baked fake players needing correction, who've been seething with scars of malfeasance
Fueled with no lack of pretence, the stench of their crimes overshadows tense times!

Once creedance ruled an organization of stature,
it's now suffered infiltration within by internal capture.
An infernal paralysis needing analysis thus exposing and deposing diseased Pharisees fallen from rapture
Steeped in querulous charades engaged in a spurious narrative of Russian intrusion!
An illusion spawning confusion of some who can't quite see clearly, too dumb to perceive these parasites inciting riot who'd be saner if quiet!
But the aplomb of troubled souls is often sullied by moles and trolls in our society intent to feed impropriety!
Not choosing to breed piety and allegiance, thereby attaining the clarity of truth manifesting its inherent charity, nullifying those consumed with temerity to hide such crimes of severity!
They will stop at nothing, defying real facts which when unearthed intact deny their spurious narratives

Cloaked in lying with ominous spying unleashed by an administration seething with insidious disruption
Who'd stop at nothing to destroy a man aligned with democracy intent on exposing massive hypocrisy!
Elected fairly in 2016, supported by those not dumbfounded but well grounded within charity of clarity
Who've fought back to save our republic from the brink of destruction by those consumed in corruption!

Barrack Hussein Obama the fake head of this snake, a fallen man consumed with false power and greed
Content to feed his own ego, a personal negative shadow fueled by internal demons resistant to reason,
Like Hillary Clinton leading those astray as lemmings to their own destruction within this infused eruption,
Flagrantly strutting about on stages defined by their colossal personas duly defined by such manifest lies!
Pathologically rebutting any semblance of truth to those that remain gullibly aloof to their vain spoof
Told by these idiots signifying nothing within the narrow latitude of their attitudes defined by platitudes they spew like venomous snakes we needn't endure, who seemingly can't be cured insisting they're right,
When any with insight recoil in abject horror from their presence to be shunned as spiritual peasants!
Devoid of emanating decorum manifested with adequate respect from laudable positions they infect!

INDEED! WHY OH WHY DO WE HAVE NEED OF THE CIA AND AN FBI WHO BOTH DEFY JUSTICE?
Lost In a sea of subterfuge during a deluge of obfuscation of justice basking in blatant malice of truth!
Arraigned, held at bay to convey that some are above the law where criminality flaunts its disdain, aloof!

Confident in abstaining when there is no retrieval from an organization stocked with Kremlin gremlins
Like John Brennan, Bob Mueller, James Comey, Andy McCabe or Peter Strzok, all false players running amuck
Trapped like cornered rats vainly implying the Russians colluded to sway the election of Donald Trump.
Do they think all those immune to their platitudes are deplorables with attitudes aligned with a chump?
Are they so consumed with their own stupidity or just desperate to maintain their churlish false validity?!

In fact the Democrats are the rats who conspired, mired in collusion with a Uranium One payoff infusion to The Clinton Foundation,
A money laundering cesspool which would dwarf the Mafia's by equation!
Likewise acts of treason that Obama perpetrated thinking himself immune to deception and commission.
Getting a handle on the level of scandal, it's truly astonishing going far beyond reasonable admonishing!
Can the rule of law survive any more haranguing
when past treasonable offences often justified hanging?
Or at the very least long prison sentences, so by utilizing common sense with no offensive false pretense, shouldn't phony men like Brennan be confined?
Along with Mueller a bag man in Uranium one payoff sins, determined to smother and keep under cover
The false pretense of the actual Russian collusion events!
By his investigation deception invoked and cloaked by Hillary, both fully consumed within ballooned egos
victims of their own false strategos!
Likewise a corrupt justice department is also complicit in such illicit, malicious, dereliction of duty that ISIS gunrunning operation atrocity Benghazi was the end result of, from fallen players like Eric Holder

And Loretta Lynch who's a cinch that she was also compromised by Bill Clinton's insidious tarmac collusion
Rendering Hillary's rightful prosecution to diffusion of a misappropriated illusion!

James Comey's another sold out dope along with a false pope, two more pompous detractors of humanity,
Victims of false vanity they may be painted as calamities in history remaining mysteries unto themselves
Content to be shelved as detractors from greater humanity playing bad actors rather than benefactors!
Urging some more stoically contemplative to be perceptually aligned with those heroically demonstrative,
As Donald Trump may be destined to be painted in future eras more elevated and elated!
Partnered in prosperity for all, not willing to fall for the foibles of personal gain within games some play
Who've allowed their high selves to be corrupted, shrouded in sin having no shame!
Placing bets from false fame faltered, sacrificed on its own altar being enticed by vices claimed
Sown from vain, shallow behavior no longer acting as saviors to ourselves and others as brothers!

Instead redefining ourselves when aligned
by higher spirits confided in, maintaining our life's courses
Away from sinful acts which only betray and detract
from more Godlike paths which if practiced,
Will surely nurture more flowers to shower down upon us,
as providence abounds resounding!
So that when called back to our essence above,
our presence will shine brightly as doves who preached peace,
Content to release all the attachments we made when our bodies fade, leaving legacies conveyed truly benevolently made!

Titled: 9 pm 8/17/18. Conceived & transmitted by Jeff Forman @ 9:30 am-12:40 pm October 11th, 2018.

Lines 19-24 conceived & transmitted between 3:25-3:43 pm and 3:55 pm on October 11th, 2018

Page 2 Subtitle + next 3 lines 25-27 conceived @1:20-1:50 pm on July 15th, 2016 ALL RIGHTS RESERVED.

Typed & edited with difficulty & a few short breaks between 12:00 am-7:25 am on November 2nd, 2018.

BIG PHARMAS CANCER INDUSTRY PROTOCOL— FORESTALLED AND RECALLED

Line those sickly bodies up against the wall
for our tried and true protocol, let's have a ball!
It's one size fits all whether fat, thin, short or tall
what we offer isn't small, just colossal gal!
Inflating our egos lining our pockets,
our false strategos will knock your eyes out of their sockets!
Let's deflate your health to increase our wealth,
our voodoo science operates well within stealth.
No natural cures offered to this day to make your cancer go away,
For that would drain our coffers playing a sane game
not prolonging your stay, allowing your getaway
From our vast array of drugs, dispensed and purveyed by thugs,
who bask in immunity with no recompense, lacking common sense!
Feeding such immense gloom enlarging the tomb of dying souls
who meekly enroll in our satanic payroll!
Within a guise of caring we loom disguised sharing ill gotten gains,
no shame as we stain those unclear with paralyzing fear!
Never allowing natural cures to endure
much less endowing benevolent prophets to cultivate allure!
Rest assured we must ensure to shut them down from any renown,
for we can't profit nor afford having them around, for their profound
approaches just might be sound and truly astounding
Thus destined throughout the world resounding,
dumfounding our cockroach claims as diabolical games!
Perpetuated by some criminally insane, so profane and vain
their high selves became shelved forced to cower

Within towers erected unframed from truth by those truly aloof,
inflamed with the gain of false fame
By many unruly who've cruelly stained our society with gross
impropriety, lacking in piety imbued by sin, infected within!
Who must be arraigned and held accountable,
none privy to deferred defense council nor formerly redoubtable
with prosecution insurmountable!
All former dread now rendered dead,
no shred of evidence left unearthed, ill-gotten birth immersed
Within eternal curses of those misguided who never confided
with the masses as crass examples of outright asses!
That wallowed like piglets in sties of their own making baking
falsehoods, forever taking from those quaking profoundly aching!
No longer shaking, now soundly rejoicing in choices they're voicing
founded in clarity infused by charity!

Conceived & transmitted by Jeff Forman @6:12-7:32 pm. Typed & tweaked @8:15-10:15 pm October 17th, 2018. ALL RIGHTS RESERVED. Written in free flow inspired from watching The Truth About Cancer:
A Global Quest Episode 8 on 10/17 paused @ 30 minutes in to write my draft as noted above. One of Dr. Burzynski's patients Arize Chris Oneekwar was diagnosed with colon cancer 8 years ago by doctors at Harmen Memorial & M. D. Anderson Hospitals in Houston Texas who adamantly told him that surgery was his only option (inspiring the line one size fits all in my poem). Instead he opted to proceed with the individualized treatment that Dr. Burzynski's clinic offered instead of going through conventional treatment first as some of his relatives advised him to do. Yet bureaucrats & lawyers acting on behalf of the industry harass and try to destroy Dr. Burzynski's career and others who he aptly states should be rewarded for their ingenuity representing the vanguard and the cutting edge of real healing & cures!

THE OBAMA ADMINISTRATION UNDERGOES AN OVERDUE CORRECTION AS ITS MASSIVE DECEPTION HAS BEEN BREACHED WITH THE DEBACLE OF BENGHAZI UNLEASHED, FAST & FURIOUS UNCLOAKED, ALL PERPETRAITORS HELD ACCOUNTABLE NO LONGER JUSTICE INSURMOUNTABLE NOR REVOKED!

The wicked witch in The Wizard of Oz had claws
dispatched with winged vengeance by monkey's paws!
If you dare speak revealing the lies of this demonic freak
you may succumb to her bag of deadly treats
A date with fate by this former secretary of state,
crossing this hag's path you'll be assailed by her wrath!
Did plans fail with Ambassador Stevens impaled,
shut in coffin nailed by Benghazi's arranged blood bath?
Henchman Obama aloof and detached, no cavalry dispatched
thus four valiant not saved by absent chivalry.
Zounds the proof abounds testimony states
that this triumvirate of fate had a date with their spawn ISIS,
The Fast and Furious gun running operation
that Eric Withholder was shunning in clear dereliction of duty!
Cloaking the truth which led to border agent Brian Terry's death,
chalk up success to this ruthless mess of thieves,
Many souls raked over the coals fanned with wicked plans
by this snake headed Gorgon!

Will this be the final siren song of Hillary's shrill shillery, her pillory prepared being finally ensnared by vile traps of her own making when one unwraps all the gifts she's dispatched through faking?
Raking donations via the Clinton Foundation,
naught but a paid to play laundering bank that stank with elation!
Fueled with corruption, the suction wielded yielding an eruption of givers who quivered with delight,
Their insight privy to the funnels of massive security leaks breached into the state department!
Naught but a clearing house which served as another treasonous compartment to their insatiable greed!

Seeds truly demonic for it seemed that nothing could impede this breed of vampires feeding on any innocents fleeing from lewd pedophiles feasting;
Bohemian Grove being one of many lairs of their crude iniquity, taking blood baths in satanic black mass rituals stained with children maimed by an insane propinquity for lust, thrust upon innocents enslaved in adversity with a penchant for perversity of hexed depravity!
Repulsive inhuman elation going far beyond what could be deemed mere vexation, this festering cavity Pizzagate exponentially exceeded Watergate, as Nixon's administration paled in comparison as a travesty I profess!
Dwarfed by that of the Obamination with Barry the irate fake in command, his head in the sand traps of every golf course he walked, as he flapped his lips spewing his lies dispatching his spies he relied upon
to thwart Donald Trump's election, engineering the worst highly treasonous infection of criminal acts ever dispatched with his troupe of defectors from truth,
A vile collection of twerps being very bad actors,
nefarious all in their collective fall from decency!

Being of sound mind nor unkind, I profess they're all detractors
to be banished forever for their colossal crimes
that could only be overlooked by those totally blind!
This festering collection with an insatiable, insufferable predilection
for twisting all truth, resisting any prosecution in a mockery of
justice dispensed by others in their breaches of trust, cloaked in
pretense by mad lust for impeachment of the only truly transparent
administration headed by Donald Trump, who's been a perpetual
pump for making America great again!
Kickstarting its once proud engine of prosperity
fueled by what some false ingrates would deem temerity,
in reality being unbridled alacrity feeding charity!
Freeing the constraints and complaints of many from the odious
restraints of one nefarious Barry, the false emperor of greed a truly
demonic seed along with his high priestess Hillary and designated
Wingman Holder!
Has there ever been any other bolder trifectorate impregnated with
such a propensity for colder ruthlessness fueled with the intensity
of unlimited guile and unvarnished truthlessness, which served
to beguile many less able to comprehend the complicit fake news
media, spewing it's unabashed Illicit torrent of outright lies, trash
talking our president to protect these imposters from the least
transparent administration in history!

Determined to remain a mystery and immune to being found
culpable, when evidence abounds underscoring how insufferable
their half baked, depraved, ongoing charades have been, in
vain attempts to evade the hammer of justice that pervades the
unstoppable purveyors of truth, Judicial Watch, proverbial bulldogs
of just missions, acting commissioned visionaries ever wary of
false fairies guised in predatory ways!

Never dismayed by the fakes and delays of a half baked Department of miscarriage Of Justice and egregious congress who have few willing to confess their sins, as many are unwilling to profess the truth they remain aloof from!

For that would require that they justifiably retire and expire from circulation after admission to enslaved shilling, maintaining the deception which should cost them any re-election, with little need for reflection to any not snookered by their blatant deception!

Any former oaths of office shattered, spattered with stains of far from illustrious gains in their shameful games perpetuated with disdain, guised within false fame which any decent soul would justifiably complain about and call profane!

When the smoke clears with fears overcome and dispelled the former stench will be cleansed and the smell of perfume will loom in its stead cleansing those dead from the fumes of greed and power that devoured them, their perpetrators doomed to fester within unhallowed tombs in unsound ground!

Whereas the innocents cleansed by those serving to amend and defend freedom and truth, unified will breed new wisdom from youth sowing flowers of freedom far and wide!

Bridging all gaps that sought to divide, confiding in harmony disarming all larcenous tyranny!

Doomed forever to infamy, all tombs they founded now abound resounding in givers of joyous renown!

Conceived & transmitted by Jeff Forman @11:14 am- 2:15 pm October 23rd, 2018. ALL RIGHTS RESERVED
Typed & edited with difficulty on October 30th from 3:15-9:45 am & 11:00-11:55 pm October 31st, 2018.
Original 4 line title revised between 3:15-3:40 am, November 1st with 3rd line omitted & 4th line altered.
Alternate title conceived as BENGHAZI, FAST AND FURIOUS AND PIZZAGATE: THREE DATES WITH FATE!

BUTTERFLY, HOW DO YOU FLY?

Few creatures of nature can elicit such
a sigh as the flowers grand butterfly!
True features which allure emit yearn to touch
or command of beauty one can't deny.
Do teachers of nomenclature submit much
or try to understand how they really fly?
To breeders who endure to commit thus
still stand more insight to find and supply more
New feeders to procure even a whit
and finally land the right not to buy ignored
Dew leechers enough mature to edict
sufficient demand and might to cry out for
Glue breathers who ensure as misfits
their albums stand to delight then spy upon more
Blue breachers to cure to whit
a luscious plan enacting wondrous flight in clear sky adored!
Knew preachers so pure to not evict
a grain of sand their sight doth mystify implored.

Conceived & transmitted by Jeff Forman from 4:50-5:41 pm & 6:20-6:24 pm on October
28th, 2018
Typed & tweaked with minimal editing @9:50-10:30 pm on October 28th, 2018. ALL
RIGHTS RESERVED.

BUTTERFLY

What a unique stand which commands such attention,
being far from conventional in its choice design
Any speak as fans that it withstands much retention,
breeding praise sensational no gimmicks to confine,
Or tweak one so grand it demands touch, its invention
seeding amazement no occupational limits to malign
Wire wings fanned out in grace expands enough its dimension,
yielding floral platters suspended, aligned
In wing tips extended top and bottom, painted blossoms
beckoning any butterflies I reckon pirouetting by!
More flowers abound front and back on central and external panels,
their perfumed scents resounding a cry
With enthralling calls, summoning any on wing to a rapturous ball,
compelling them all to immediately fly
In haste to embrace their perfumed faces,
thus consume any traces of their luscious fragrance, not deny
It's wafting through the air entrancing those lingering unaware,
flitting hummingbirds darting nearby,
Also prone to make the rounds, no marooned places
and social graces swift but sure with brief allure, to spy,
Like balloons hovering momentarily dancing on
defying all understanding, wondrous aeronautics spry!
Like bumblebees withstanding their own weight,
denying fate of gravity with aplomb and suitable alacrity,
Always wanton to elude ones eye, amazing all
never succumbing to a fall from flight delighting our sight!
Astounding hummingbirds don't sing, beating wings resound
surprisingly unlike meanders of butterflies.

Conceived and transmitted for Stand #53 for Scandleglass Creations for Enlightenment by Jeff Forman @7:30-9:10 pm on October 28th, 2018. ALL RIGHTS RESERVED
Typed with time consuming editing challenges from 11 pm Oct.28th, 2018-1:00 am October 29th, 2018 to fit & largely retain initial draft content within the spatial limitations of Microsoft Office Word 2007.

FALSE ASPIRATIONS CLEANSED BY US MAKING AMENDS

No shame means no gain for some seeking false acclaim,
Along with some who court fame who seem willing to refrain
From indulging in rigged games which make claims upon their souls
Leaving stains like varicose veins which take their fair share of tolls!

Like burrowing moles and trolls who undermine stability,
no regard for civility;
Their agility quite limited, committed in stealth
being encumbered by false wealth
Comes senility likely with inhibited health,
as high selves slumber with this hand dealt!

Some withstand such abuse
succumbing to misuse they stand against the truth,
Internal command much confused
numbing to infuse feigned self surrendered aloof!
How much unvarnished proof will be required
to strip the tarnish they've acquired?
Out of touch unfinished youth became attired
equipped within a harness they've admired;
The clout of such diminished truth well mired,
unless they confess to paths aspired that they sired!
With doubt in touch evidenced proof conspired,
undressed as louts seen mean expired,
The spout of providence forsooth rewired,
professed shouts those keen foretell inspired!

None without ample presence to recuse
from some former exasperates who refused to lose
They used and abused, too confused
to allow false selves fostered to be plastered over as imposters!
Who walked upon stages throughout prolonged ages,
squandering their own internal sages,
As they stalked more game in eternal engages
of their fellow man, victims of infernal rampages!
Rejects of their own clan, until a plan restores the ages
of fair bellow to fan respect from ones neglected,
All those infected renounced, and eternally rejected,
all false air hallowed, now universally disinfected!

Conceived and transmitted by Jeff Forman from 12:00 midnight-1:24 am on November 16th, 2018
Typed with minimal editing & revisions from 1:25-2:30 am November 16th, 2018 ALL RIGHTS RESERVED.

A NOTION FOR MASTERING THE COMMOTION OF CONFLICTING EMOTIONS USING DEVOTION

When the commotions caused by negative emotions
seemingly beyond control take their toll
on those sensitive, we must learn to pause
as sagely mentors to our tempers and thus extol
Attentiveness to yearn to applaud our noble virtues
disarming those progressively stern
Back to harmony from harming thereby alarming our inner guides
who preside and will confide
If we can learn to abide by their override in arming our innate,
truly immense, sanctified sense
In potentially guarding against our sinners pride
which seeks to divide us from those meek
Who must be stern and speak out during trying times
to those oppressive with shallow minds,
Their thrust to burn ones they see as lesser and confine,
just because their shout is less aggressive,
From a more hallowed inner space that they've embraced
having faced up to their real potential
Fueling their emotions as utensils which can often place them
on shaky ground, while giving them options
To become more sound in actions taken more profound,
replacing rash tendencies for crass behavior
To be redesigned, as civil saviors to themselves
and others realigned, as soulful sisters and blood brothers
Under various skins, immune to its predilections to be rather thin
when pricked by the unwitting pins

Of some nefarious who aren't so hilarious
when deemed quite contrarious by those less inhibited
Exhibiting esteemed insight who've mastered the art
of cultivating contrite, to nullify any more petty
Who are quick to fight, their lowered frequency nullifying
their reset potential for decorum and decency
This must be prioritized sequentially as essential
to elevate all human beings to their higher potential!
So that none become ingrates who salivate for more,
quick to close the door of humane understanding
Which if left ajar enables a cogent commanding presence
to neutralize pretence and any preponderance
To feel superior to sisters and brothers they decide
to trample down as inferiors, content to divide
In stark contrast to ones who shirk the dark within their souls
which can dim their own awareness of sin,
So they can abide making their mark to confide in each other
with unified strength to smite down kin
Who want to smother, their cover laid bare
now exposed in their lairs for all to gaze at such ones in haze!
Who've reached such depths of despair
they're bereft of reason, impaired within their own sterile space
Where they've sought to embrace and erase all sense of compassion,
rendered dense unwilling to face
That exerting ones passion for flying flags of reason
is never outmoded fashion nor out of season!
Such that any and all spying erodes freedom,
thus it must be vanquished and banished forever
Along with those conniving who are lying in treason,
acting as levers to potentially sever all fair unity
With immunity to any aligned community
which can only be sought and never bought with impunity!

Or radical schemes that can only destroy true self esteem
rendering those fallen to be deemed unclean!
No longer fit for redeemed service such tainted purpose
of worthless renown, ill spent to astound and
Thus confound their own inner guides who just can't break through
the din of their constricting sins
That permeated their skin as they've deafened within
to all voices aligned with more noble choices!
Can we save ones content to enslave
who've mortgaged themselves to hell 'cause the knell that quelled
Their internal moral compass has become encompassed
with constricting emotions?
No mind's eye clear to dispel the fear and repel the sneer
of the eternal external commotion which has confused their lives
To a point of no return to source, their only recourse
to infuse the thrust of their lives to not be contrived,
Rather purified by loving awareness, no fairness denied
to all of mankind realigned unified In God We Trust!

Conceived and transmitted by Jeff Forman from 2:54-4:45 pm on November 16th, 2018.
1st 3 lines & 4th line through harming were written from 3:28-3:35 pm on November 9th,
2018. ALL RIGHTS RESERVED.
Typed & tweaked with some minor revisions & additions intermittently between 9:40
pm November 18th (when titled) & 2:40 am November 19th, 2018.

WILL THE THRUST OF OUR CURRENT SOCIETY EVER BREAK THROUGH THE CRUST OF IMPROPRIETY FUELED BY MISTRUST OF THOSE TOO SHORTSIGHTED TO BE JUST?

If we learned by our mistakes perhaps we could embrace
our reason and thus replacing all acts of treason,
If we yearned to not be fakes in traps that would disgrace,
empowered reason commands trust defacing cataracts of heathens;
If we discerned so none partakes as saps we should replace,
sound reason withstands thrust embracing facts of grievance,
When some deceive false stakes entraps true livelihood displaced,
cowered reason demands unjust misplacing tracts of bereavement;
Societies come and go, yet despite how much we curry reason
its crust retracing impacts all new seasons
Propriety's sum remains the same in this tired game,
still out of touch blurry reason can't understand much mistaking
retracts some demons!

There always is one faction that's intent upon distraction
who invariably gain some traction to others resisting retraction,
Their progress remains impacted ever bent and thus contracted
never clever forever infected immune to being properly corrected,
Their minds aligned confined, forever compliant to the status quo
reliant, too weak to be defiant to dethrone their giant
Who towers over their collective sullied by a tacit invective,
nullifying any corrective as an antidote to the yoke which chokes
them like a rope,

Retaining their disdain to make a change
and thus refrain from playing dumb to their aplomb,
Instead renouncing their mistrust breaking through its crust,
trouncing its fair share of rust no longer a glare to becoming just!
So unjust becomes unclean, when formerly unseen
it was just a scheme lacking appropriate sheen
like a forgotten dream, now truly gleaned!
No longer covered and left smothered by their former collective
set free, with corrective high selves unshelved compelled,
duly cleaned and rendered pristine!
May we become immune to any gloom prone to entomb our room
for reason, so that the din doesn't wear thin our clarity of vision
To see beyond our own skin color
blinding us from our sisters and brothers,
we all share one another as vigilants unyielding
in commission of our shared glorious mission!

Some are so consumed with hate
it seems their current unenviable fate is to remain forever irate
In order to potentially complicate others lives they want to deny,
defying and even spying on them,
Content to rely on orchestrated schemes to short circuit dreams
and remain unclean with supreme
Streams of epic hatred that spews forth from their foul mouths
promulgated like diarrhea unabated!

In our current season of unrest many have lost touch with jest,
preferring to just vehemently detest our present POTUS
putting him on notice that impeachment is their ultimate agenda!
No reason left with which to commend them, our only recourse left
it seems to attend to them behind closed doors
where saner souls remain ignored as out to lunch,

Yet it's my hunch that this disingenuous foul bunch of dunces
are far beyond many there who remain unfound,
lost within recesses of their still unsound minds
to which they have become confined,
Many of whom nonetheless are not unkind and almost sublime
in their blunder perhaps lost in wonder, while others thunder away
in blind debasing rhetoric!
Leaving those of us saner very dismayed,
resolute in not being so vain like those so profoundly insane
whose games lusting for more power have attained
levels that their cowered souls have become devoured,
As castaways in constructed towers,
obstructed within by the confounding din of their own iniquities,
Displaying no propinquity for others
they've lost touch with their brothers, smothered by their mad egos,
Truly sad with false strategos misaligned with truth and justice
conveying venom so naught to recommend,
Bought and paid for they need to be shown the doors
of asylums to which they should be confined,
No presence of their minds left which can be redesigned
much less refined or amended and realigned!

Let's see we have Nancy Pelosi as speaker of the house
who should instead become a disinfected louse,
Confined to cackle in a perverse hen house of nut cases
who has proven averse to any reasonable bases!
And mad Maxine Waters, a very sad case who wants to erase
any claims of being sane in order to save face
Because she can only embrace her own race in blind hatred
of all that's profoundly sacred,
Naked, a castaway from her own humanity, a true calamity
consumed with her own profanity as is another, one she sees as
her sister, Michelle Obama who excels at being a blister
upon a saner society, no propriety left here content to smear

our current commander with her scowling face etched with hate
always irate!
Fated to be naught but a reprobate on history's unbiased slate
crafted with reason rather than shafted
With many counts of high treason that a former cowardly false
commander continues, his raised dander full of slander
befitting such a kook who remains aloof to any rebuke
sickening many who want to puke
When subjected to his false face soon to be erased from any claims
to a worthy legacy, rather a stain as he defamed his oath of office,
naught but a sick scurvy he brought upon it as an oaf preposterous!
Known raucously to multitudes in magnitude throughout the world
now as narcistically debaucherous.

Can greater humanity soon collectively smite and repress
the duress of these incessant pests and repossess
control from all of the Deep State moles and trolls
who've attempted to break our half baked society?
Consumed more than ever with impropriety
floundering in confounding currents of misguided people,
As astounding adherents of evil to false steeples
of idolic worship and warships which must be cast out
once and for all from their repugnant ball,
forever cast adrift and held at bay with resolute dismay!
As we redeem, redefine and realign the course of our mother ship
to smoother seas addressing all pleas
To formally appease all of the unjust suffering
restoring valuable trust by installing sufficient buffering,
To restore planet earths entire playing field
to collective harmony yielding no further disharmony,
Nor hypocrisy to mar fair democracy in governments
realigned to not use people confined as sheeple
So that we all shine as sublime mined diamonds
realigned with stellar harmony oh so divine!

First two paragraphs conceived and transmitted by Jeff Forman from 5:55-8:50 am December 15th, 2018.

Third paragraph conceived and transmitted by Jeff Forman from 4:53 pm-4:57 pm December 15th, 2018.

Rest conceived and transmitted by Jeff Forman from 5:28-6:28 pm Dec.15th, 2018. ALL RIGHTS RESERVED.

Typed with minimal editing or revisions from 10:00 pm Dec. 15th to 2:30 am on December 16th, 2018.

Written shortly after watching the 1949 movie Intruder In The Dust which was the kernel of inspiration that inspired me to write the initial 2 segments before going to bed to get some much needed sleep and then resuming with the latter segments later that day! Ultimately I was chagrined to conclude that despite the obvious anti-black racism that existed in society at that time in America's history poignantly captured in the film & the fact that we largely outgrew such blatant treatment of African Americans as 2nd class citizens since then, we now have a new current form of subtly intolerant yet pervasive discrimination in society that is actually more scrambled than ever with all the political correctness that is being foisted upon us. I respectfully but vehemently resist all forms of indoctrination which ultimately are for controlling and manipulating people's free will.

REDEEMING MEAN FROM THOSE UNCLEAN RESTORING THE SHEEN TO NEW WORLD DREAMS

If one becomes a lackey of a bully or would be tyrants,
they'd be better off becoming migrants.

If someone overcomes forces that sully what could be compliant,
they'd see fetters doffed reaping nobly defiant.

If everyone's aplomb's reinforced so no gullies sought would be
aspirant, there'd be letters stopped bleeping those non-reliant.

If free will's restored imploring no ills ignored,
we can fill explored dreams negating all unclean schemes
Restoring sheen to all keen not to snore with mean,
bored, unfulfilled shills elating false thrills, which stall if not kill
what God mercifully redeems!
May we please find insight promoting rights as keys, freeing glee
that's been confined, left unforeseen
by some rendered blind, imposing downfall of many
having become less refined, aloof to fight might,
neglecting proper respect with coffers filled sans intellect!

Forsooth may they become circumspect,
not has-beens in decline who impose stress in regress aligned,
Contrary to our inner sage, to whom we must defer
and thus confer with, to reengage our noble page
On equal ground with footing sound, enabled to astound
if left to its inherent renown to be profound!

If not disabled from diffusion, through lenses blurred
by false illusions, that tyrants foster as imposters,
Being investors in their own internal jesters of pretense,
lurking behind facades truly immense as cruel nimrods
Devoid of insight, who fight to retain false gain
of their brothers they've sullied and smothered in vain,
staining their shame which they've covered with masks of disdain
that can't hide false acclaim nor pain
When they're shocked enough to reclaim themselves,
as former goners who must restore their honor
with reclaimed, humility and civility towards others,
No longer kept in servitude, betrayed, dismayed, enslaved,
berated, negated and decimated!
Instead, elevated back to sound ground
equal in stature, fully enraptured and duly emancipated!

1st 5 stanzas conceived and transmitted by Jeff Forman from 4:11 pm-5:10 pm on December 20th, 2018.
Last 8 stanzas written by Jeff Forman from 5:24-6:00 pm on December 20th, 2018.ALL RIGHTS RESERVED.
Typed & tweaked with minimal editing from 2:40 pm-4:30 pm on December 21st, 2018.
Inspired by watching the movie Born Yesterday (1950) in which Judy Holliday repeated her Broadway triumph & won an Oscar reprising her role playing a quintessential dumb blond tutored to became cultured and educated, thus emancipated from her overbearing tyrannical partner Broderick Crawford.
I personally echo as further inspiration in crafting this poem the noble words of Thomas Jefferson referenced a 2nd time at the film's end where they're etched in a façade of a building in Washington DC. "I have sworn on the altar of God eternal hostility against every form of tyranny over the mind of man."
That profound oath fuels and compels much of my poetry which targets the huge preponderance of tyranny on display worldwide in our current society!

THE WISDOM TO SEEK DIVINITY OVERCOMING INIQUITY IN SACRIFICE TO PROPINQUITY

Oft times people's lives remain shrouded in mystery
cloaked within an overriding history
of inappropriate gain filled with stains of false fame
and its dubious accompanying acclaim
Despite crimes amidst sighs which confine clouded sin
whisper choked of being one's kin
by not confiding enduring blisters by refrain stilled with shame
within the strifes of life's tepid game.

The bite of fright chimes when fate makes a date
to come calling as some succumb falling dead
Others stray in dismay as an array of (re)actions arises
with some donning misguided disguises
Attired as such requires compromises in their life's path,
in the wake of fate's wrath their staff
becomes bent, with resolve somewhat spent
they choose to relent in quests more heaven sent,
despite appropriate repent they didn't resent enough
to snuff the appeal of vice which can entrap them,
despite its many shades that entice some don't withstand
the fight which inevitably saps their reservoirs of contrite,
their self-reliance impaired in flight from right
as wrong becomes the tune of their song.
Aplomb likewise also fails to go along with this path taken,
many noble heartfelt dreams thus forsaken!

As sacrifices made become stock in trade more duly conveyed,
fully displayed with high selves betrayed
Their inlaid presence now eroded, rendered reticent peasants
like worn down rocks their field diffused
With confidant's stock confused their enrollment abused,
displaced as former flocks of one now clothed
within far more fancier frocks which can't hide her curse
to abide within her torment of sin, of one she nursed
alone in stealth given up to legitimate wealth & standing
to nurture a life to be one commanding.
Neither sullied nor stained via false gains or acclaims,
no evil claims upon his soul with free will inspired
to raise him up higher to lofty goals in which he enrolled,
sired in stability with agility not mired within a fragility of life
steeped in strife that often can seem like a curse or worse
if one's available purse support is sufficiently lacking,
in surrender forced to endure a shellacking
of the sheen of their high self's esteem
unable to preen away the tarnish of a former varnish, adopted
in deference to an unbounded motherly reverence she opted
to forsake in silence, allowing the full vengeance of the law
to partake of her life rather than inflict any undo strife
on another she sired as a dutiful mother,
whose once quaking, aching, breaking heart
made the loftiest sacrifice in dwarfing all of her erstwhile vice,
giving us all experiencing life the wisdom to ponder that its most
noblest reward may be redeemed not by paths squandered,
but perhaps by those well beyond our human understanding
that loom far above the limited commanding
our earthly sight can procure, forever enduring in the radiant allure
esteemed with angelic renown astounding us beckoning yonder
to our universal maker and founder
on our soul's eventual re-encounter!

Transmitted and conceived by Jeff Forman @ 5:25-8:25 pm on January 7th, 2019. ALL RIGHTS RESERVED.

Directly inspired by viewing the classic William A. Wellman film Frisco Jenny (1933) for the second time.

Typed & tweaked with minor editing & additions between 1:00 am-5:00 am on January 18th, 2019.

EXPOSING AND DEPOSING ALL FALSE MASTERS, RESTORING US ALL TO CLEANER GREENER HEAVENLY PASTURES!

The puppet masters lurk and smirk behind the scenes
Intent upon felling those with nobler dreams!
They trumpet disasters to displace turf and besmirch ones kind,
Their schemes hell bent beyond quelling,
To depose truth tellers of singular means and minds!
Intent upon twisting fate by promulgating hate
within ones already predisposed to being irate,
No longer willing to procrastinate their impulses towards crassness
or being privy to sound debate.
For cooler and wiser heads cannot prevail
When baseless agitators avail themselves of faceless tales
Which impose the wrath of their witless users,
deemed convenient nitwits and confusers.
Retained as misers to contrivers of divisive missions to incite,
Assailed with faceless perpetrators of fright
berserkly wielding might against those possessing clearer insight!
And thus division is the essence of these crafters sustenance,
Perched within treacherous rafters as grafters one and all
who enthrall within their infernal, eternal balls!
Creating schism at the expense of those contrite
who are more immune to ignite their inner spite,
Retaining recompense of such extent to prevent
extortion of those with sinners pride content to deride
ones more apt to confide in saintly endeavors
who engage in using clever as a benevolent lever!

Exerting force emanating from the heart
as an unlimited resource pure, thus able to endure
any tests those pests from the ruling class unleash
to increase their impure and unjust forceful ways,
only causing dismay in their array of webs
to convey those more naive, dead in their cycles of dread!
Forever now exposed as abject dreams
in schemes of some to extol darkness,
The starkness of their mortgaged souls eroding,
stripped of their true wealth,
perhaps unwittingly chipped within stealth
to eternal debasement of their spiritual health!
Which once squandered or laundered can no longer be
extended or amended within God's rightful plans,
which never fall short of those heeding its noble commands!
No matter how many grains of sand traverse the hourglass,
Those who retain the true majesty of the upper class
are never so crass as to subjugate others,
by smothering themselves under the covers of illusion
to promote confusion without,
When it's them who are condemned to eternal dilution within,
because of sins they've embraced, rather than sought to erase
by becoming heartfeltly repentant!
Thus restoring the sheen to their souls once again washed clean,
with nothing now left unseemly much less unseen,
to instill all towards universal heavenly dreams!

Conceived & transmitted by Jeff Forman @2:35 am-3:10 am/titled at 4:27 am on February 4th, 2019.
Inspired viewing the film The Avenger (1962) with Steve Reeves paused at 53:00. Expediently written.
Typed faithfully from rough draft during early am of March 27th/28th, 2019. ALL RIGHTS RESERVED.

THE SCOPE OF FREE WILL CAN ROPE US INTO DEMONIC POSSESSION OR COAX US INTO DIVINE PROTECTION AND THUS UNIVERSAL RESURRECTION!

God grants us freewill, so it's up to us to instill the wisdom to fulfill
our holy doctrine, thou shalt not kill our spiritual will!
It shouldn't be confined,
nor sacrilegiously re-aligned with demonic possession,
which can certainly thwart ones potential resurrection,
much less distort any pious confession!
Yet that couldn't be refined to ensure correction
for sometimes defection is the remedy with infection
As we compel ourselves to the knell of a justifiable hell,
which repels any cure unless we can endure
the allure of the dark in order to spark a new found reality,
when the starkness of morality enlightens the duality
of human existence, thus consuming resistance
to re-focusing on the light with enriched insight!
Illuminating the night, pitching the might that resists contrite with spite,
For the fight's not really with others,
who when seen clearly are our sisters and brothers,
who all can embrace as part of our singular human race!
No factions to erase with captions which disgrace,
restoring allure with our essences pure so we can collectively ensure
that we will endure to procure a new found wealth!
No longer stockpiled in stealth by a rabid elite
who revel in deceit with lives callously incomplete,
Their defeat is now certain, as their final curtain calls enthrall few!

For none can forestall those true to their own moral compass,
It trumpets the call far and wide, that when we all collectively abide
by our own gestalt to correct all our faults,
No vault is too wide for us to not leap such false divide,
with all will coalesced melting any former resisting distress!
Attesting to those who embrace their best,
no further need to confess our sins
when a collective din of restored kin
no longer pricks our universal skin
ensconced within as none wander without!
Our hearts and souls stalwart and stout,
All pout refined realigned in clarity of universal parity,
None left to founder with mistrust in unjust temerity or disparity!

Conceived and transmitted by Jeff Forman from 4:11 am-5:14 am on February 28th, 2019.
Typed with no editing from 5:05 am-6:45 am March 26th, 2019. ALL RIGHTS RESERVED.

THE RANCID CANCER OF NEGLECT THAT'S ACHIEVED BY RETAINING POLITICALLY CORRECT!

Please excuse my abject dismay
which I'm sometimes compelled to convey
when my internal sage becomes duly enraged,
sans recuse a proper parley
over misfits who off-times excel with gross display
in their smug diatribes against those of a cast-out tribe
deemed politically incorrect, whose only real crimes are having
the audacity and capacity to be devout enough to speak out!
Against those whose only real clout
is how much they prop up their external lout
to contort their own internal sin within,
which must be kept in check by their ongoing neglect,
stained with malfeasance maintained
to attain their propped up spurious fame!
As aligned audiences in precipitous decline
continue to whine, devoid of their own moral spines
they continue to spew their maligning hate,
some reprobates who just can't shirk the looming fate
of their infernal, enraged irate,
Dooming them to a future karma,
sometimes destined to even supporting Big Pharma
that's always glad to enslave more of those sad,
misaligned in decline to postures supine!
Rendering their countenances contorted, pugnaciously etched
in retaining politically correct views which they spew,
more and more crude and outlandish
as they brandish their arsenal of deceit!

Woe be it for them whose phlegm fosters
their roster of ongoing impostors,
Spewing hypocrisy defaming true democracy
when all are heard, even those deemed turds
by those who run roughshod with the herd!
They're truly absurd when stripped of their repugnant facades,
equipped with veneers so austere that any of us clear
should never fear to confront them with the affronts they present!
Thereby blunting these churlish, impish louts,
calling them out as Doubting Thomas's,
strident thugs who must be proverbially clubbed into submission
and reviled with ughs retained for their putrid submissions,
emitted by emissaries of hate
who have sealed their own fates with obsolescence!

An unwitting gallery of adolescents such as Rachel Maddow,
a sour tart whose ongoing verbal stench is truly immense
and must surely add more greenhouse gasses to our atmosphere
than all of the farts from cows we endear!

Then there's Bill Mayer, whose very image should evoke despair,
and disgust for one who enthralls so much in his own love affair
with himself, no heartfelt reserve ever felt or dealt,
nor contemplated to limit his elated, rancid, candid smirking,
lurking behind his overgrown proboscis thrust upon us,
truly far from an Adonis!

Dens of iniquity such as CNN and MSNBC,
bastions of deceit replete with staffs demonstrating
no apparent limits to the levels of their searing, spurious banter,
so quick to canter with the malicious cancer
that spews from the fake veneer of their false facades
bereft of any endearing accolades!

These collective affronts should render anyone sane to ruefully
eschew the heartburn and cacophony of their foundering domain,
compiled from a rampant disdain for truth,
so they can continue aloof
resonating in decline, confined to refrain
in their game from any claim other than to defame others,
vile traitors to their own sisters and brothers!
Blisters unto themselves smothering their high selves
to the tragedy of all in their fall from grace,
erasing their own future prosperity
wallowing in the lower vibrational disgrace of their own temerity,
lacking clarity of useful service and purpose,
destined to be shelved within the archaic annals of history as worthless!

So sad their submission is so complete
that they don't perceive the attrition they've reaped
by the severity of their own shortcomings,
be they sins of commission or omission!
May they one day still awaken to new horizons, where
service to others is bequeathed to those who are truly uplifting,
not weighed down with graft or defaming wrath
by others smothered for callously sifting,
For they themselves could be eclipsed
from a greater humanity's harmonized future
Which will only bestow accolades upon those
with countenances cultivated and steeped in allure with virtue!

Conceived & Transmitted by Jeff Forman from 2:05-4:56 pm, May 4th, 2019. ALL RIGHTS
RESERVED. Typed and tweaked with some editing and revision between 7:30 pm-11:30
pm. Titled at 1:54 pm.

THE ULTIMATE WEALTH FOR ONE'S SPIRITUAL HEALTH ALIGNING WITH SOURCE AS THE ULTIMATE RESOURCE

Too much wealth acquired in stealth
is not a recipe for one's spiritual health!
Often it eventually becomes a burden,
softening the resolve of many a person
Like a millstone hung around their necks,
it counteracts all that disinfects
As a yoke placed upon a pair of oxen,
it sullies one's will like a tedious toxin!
When used as such it abuses much,
like the tainted touch of a Midas rush!
It hardens all that its contact befalls,
including all free will that's innately instilled!
Turned within, churned with malice into sin
these contracts do not forestall what their users invoke
For they're the dopes around whose necks
constricting ropes have fallen, restricting conflicting scopes
of reason fermented enough to turn to treason,
Their debauchery becomes a mockery of all
that was once held dear, for now fear
has become their master, the jeer of this insidious tasker
only yields more tears for those provoked,
stoked with disaster at their helms ever aging faster without!
Their internal din never ceasing, ever increasing it forces
their hands across all lands they scheme and deem to possess,
The realms they inhabit and infest are far from blessed!

Just as those politically correct,
the limitations they attempt to inflict
are laced with contempt, not meant to enrich!
Embracing conflict with egos mired in malevolence
rather than actions steeped in benevolence!
Their purpose continues to fester like mirthless jesters
who've become worthless investors in idioms based in perfidious!
Any who choose to act so insidious besmirch
their own future paths with the allure of fake trappings!
The gaps in perceived material stature, fueling much
false enrapture only shrouds their higher purpose!
For those superficial gains have only widened the distance
from their internal sages ultimate mission whose own salvation
is cultivated in those tasks embraced yielding amalgamation
of all of humanity where any division is renounced as insanity!
Thus restoring connection to source as the ultimate resource,
which only serves to enforce that which empowers all,
in their call to serve all towards eternal enthrall!

Conceived & transmitted by Jeff Forman from 1:05-3:00 pm on June 1st, 2019. ALL RIGHTS RESERVED.
Titled at 3:05 pm June 1st, 2019. Typed and formatted from 12:00 am to 2:10 am on June 12th, 2019.

MAINTAINING SAVING FACE
TO FOREGO DISGRACE

As human beings we've lived in many complex societies
that are ever changing, as there's constant rearranging
of how things are run and how they are done,
Yet the current proprieties abound with what is deemed sound!

It's enough to confound or even dumbfound any,
no matter how profound or uncanny their renown!
When former illustrious schools have been bought,
to promote certain thought wrought upon us,
Aligned with some industrious who've sought to erase
all formal debate so that they can save face
to forego the disgrace of advocating positions being proven unsound
When those with clearer unbiased reason rebound
with uninhibited perception promoted
To neutralize those caught in the trap of political correction
which lurks behind its base of outright deception,
aloof from their own cogent, coherent reception!

They staunchly maintain their defection as a deflection
of positions which might undermine their commissions!
Just like corporations could be docked their appropriations
wangled notoriously by corrupt administrations
That attempt to run roughshod over any and all opposition
Who they view with contempt and seek to abuse with acts of attrition
no matter how much blood money's infused
to eliminate all justifiable competition!
For how dare they try to upgrade a dying system
with obsolete paradigms contrived to confine,
unwind and render benign any and all
who oppose the status quo who are so gauche to be pro Freedom,
contrary to those who want to continually bleed 'em!

That's been their stock in trade to fleece the masses
forever seen as inferior classes, to reap their harvest
as they continue to preen this convenient starve chest
Which has been inflicted upon many civilizations constantly conflicted!
With savage wars ruthlessly pitting them against one another,
truthlessly succumbing always kept off balance,
So as to not recognize their own sisters and brothers,
smothered in unison within attritious, vicious confusion
that's ben naught but an orchestrated illusion!

For once the masks are torn off, the masses
will be freed to rebound, propelled with sound thought!
Formerly forlorn faces now doffed,
gleefully galvanized towards a unifying, dignified future sought!
No longer conflicted nor bought by those now disgraced,
miscreant few oligarchs they ruefully scoff!
Who can no longer seek refuge from this deluge of reason
Promoting a new season of prosperity for all,
Where none will enthrall much less prevail over the downfall of (m)any,
to callously maintain their places of false governing
with willful acts of smothering,
Snidely maintaining illusion via invoked confusion
in order to save their own face(s) to forego certain disgrace(s)!
Once our societies have solidified in just balance,
with renouncement of all who've deliberately or unwittingly
fostered false paradigms of contrived devolution
at the expense of a wizened populous,
Now exuberant, jubilant in unison with their embrace
of a universal society evolved, where the only disgrace
will be to those who don't don countenances etched
within enlightened faces of truth, fostered and nurtured in youth,
destined to abound and astound with renown
for all who've answered the call from the light,
guided with unhampered insight for right!

Conceived & transmitted by Jeff Forman from 3:09 -4:46 pm on June 8th, 2019. ALL RIGHTS RESERVED.
Titled 1:15 pm on May 4th, 2019. Typed with minor editing from 2:25 am-4:40 am on June 12th, 2019.

USING OBSERVATIONS OF HOLLY AS A GUIDE TO KEEP LIFE JOLLY BEING MINDFUL OF THE TRAP BASE EMOTIONS CAN PLAY CREATING FOLLY

The mighty prickle of its barbed leaves thistles,
might cause us to heed the need not wanting to bleed,
that we must trust to not wantonly thrust our bodily parts
within its domain which may cause us pain and sour our smiles;
Proving that any interaction beyond our optic satisfaction
can turn the jolly visual appeal of the lovely holly,
into one's more tactile distasteful folly
forcing us to reflect as we gasp golly!

We can indeed deck our halls divinely during festive Christmas seasons,
with good cause to carol in unison our gratitude for many sound reasons
which abound, as we count our many blessings
which hopefully far exceed our need
to reflect upon the years regrets,
Thus causing us to inject any humble confessions
as the result of any erstwhile transgressions
we've unwittingly inflicted upon our fellow humans,
When not seeing clearly with mindful thoughts
yielding actions kindly and words sincerely from the heart,
not allowing baseless emotions to take command
when overwrought by hurling darts!

Thus throwing sand into our inner sagely wheels of guidance,
which will always provide for our needs to humbly confide within,
to temper the din of our daily assaults,

transforming them into somersaults as we tactfully sidestep or vault,
the many pitfalls of life which can often act as a blight
projecting us rashly into flight or unleashing spite to fight with others,
Rather than reflecting on insight
to channel our thoughts as we become more of the boss!
Not yielding to cross when our delicate skin is pricked
with rash convictions within that might have once
provoked our own sass when we reacted with crass,
too swiftly revoking our reason by remembering that
the only barbs we project are when emotions aren't kept in check!
As we learn to reflect before we inject to protect all
from the need to confess or molest!

So thus more days we yearn to convey our innate charm,
as we learn it's the best antidote for harm!
Just as we've learned how to keep
our interactions with holly always jolly,
Not allowing any too close less mindful interactions to rashly put
us off guard by squandered reason and thus be rendered folly!

Conceived & transmitted by Jeff Forman from 12:05-1:31 pm on June 12th, 2019. Titled @ 11:57 pm
Typed with some minor editing & revisions from 10:04 pm-11:45 pm. ALL RIGHTS RESERVED.

A REMEDY TO DIFFUSE DECEPTION BEFORE ITS UNHOLY INCEPTION

In times of duplicitous outright deception
What is required to remedy such plight is simply insight
Restoring balance by correction with inspired convection!

Diffusing the insurmountable by infusing ones accountable
To foreclose those that are so vain who impose their ghastly reign
from a domain that's so profane, it surely must be deemed insane!

In retrospect as cosmic sleuths
can we inspect and fundamentally dissect
how such oppressors came to power,
by exercising judicious circumspect
That will reflect advance premonition
warning us against those who defect
to any stance that emboldens some
to devour those more meek who cower,
and thus grovel in hovels overshadowed
by false towers wrought by any bought,
ignorant enough to have been sought
to cultivate defiance of such unholy an alliance!
Inherently so remiss as to dismiss
their own preponderance for attrition
by preposterous commissions
infused with such intoxicating perdition!

How can we contemplate as resolute empaths such cures to endure,
Thus forewarning any from willfully treading down such desolate paths
Where they will seek to procure such rancid power,
rendering their souls so sour
they'll be compelled to surrender such enticement
null and void, a must to avoid!
Before perchance some dream and scheme
to adopt any actions so unclean and mean
to violate the sanctity of all life, forestalling strife
inflicted by false might devoid of insight!
Which those contrite never lose
by their connection to what's right, nurtured by the light!

Inspired after viewing the film The Inspector General (1949) starring Danny Kaye.
Conceived & transmitted by Jeff Forman from 2:38 am-4:07 am, June 18th, 2019.
Typed with minor editing and revisions from 10:40 pm-11:45 pm. ALL RIGHTS
RESERVED.

ARE WE WILLING TO
POTENTIALLY UNLEASH
A CHILLING TECHNOLOGY
INSTILLING THE RELEASE OF
THE UNWITTING ADVENT
OF HUMANITY'S EVENTUAL
EXTINCTION? OR WILL WE
AWAKEN IN TIME TO THE
NIGHTMARE OF THIS INSIDIOUS
CRIME RESTORING OUR SUBLIME
EMINENT DISTINCTION!

How many civilizations have come and gone is something both
archaeologists and scientists collectively ponder upon.
Deciphering clues they attempt to use to infuse some sense
into mysteries abounding and confounding which loom that are
still truly immense
Shaping catastrophic events throughout earth's history, oft times
so intense to doom a cultures constituents to such an extent
with what was unleashed that they've ceased to exist!
Ever obscured within the mists of lost times, perhaps only cursorily
defined within the whine of civilizations discontent
Which unfolds and regresses as wisdom ebbs and flows in human
beings frequent excesses, as their ultimate test
to advance with prudence or falter and regress
When their unbridled arrogance asserts it's stance within the
entrancement of entrenched benign supposed advancement

Which alters a future steeped in the allure of pretence, disguised within a false cure we must unwittingly endure to procure latent reason

Which in hindsight lends (us) insight into what instilled our plight by unleashing the blight which we then have to amend and fight to defend against its unruly might!

Replete with a grueling admission that our collective path was tainted by its ill conceived ideology imposing a cultural topography

Which we must befittingly successfully navigate from to extricate ourselves, thereby exposing and deposing its inherent czars demagoguery.

I fervently submit to all who have not succumbed to this insidious enchanting entrancement, far from any enhancement

That the current path our society relentlessly pursues, imbued with the ever increasing catastrophic, obsessive compulsive enslavement of technological devices, so fully enticing many with few resistant

That we are ever quickly devolving on the fast track to human extinction via artificial intelligence, rather than solving this dilemma with the distinction to diffuse this phantom

That abuses our own DNA and spiritual health
which it assaults via ever increasing demonic stealth!

Will our collective, remiss of denying the illicit spying
and stupefying destructive 5G bliss of our own DNA
be the final straw and fatal flaw

Of our current society lacking the sufficient piety to deflect
our trajectory away from becoming the 21st century's Atlantis?

Or will we unify collectively to incite all of our wisdom and might, guided by our Godly insight away from a flight to doom
on a revised trajectory aligned back to the light of our souls.

Which are our ultimate saviors in piloting our own behavior
to reap the rewards of universal delight!

Reactivating our ancient, dormant stargates to redefine and align humanity with those more fully evolved and guided by Godly insight Who watch and wait in their hopes that we not only survive, but thrive and mature beyond our apparent infancy nourishing the roots of our wisdom to attain the fruits of blissful consistency!

Conceived & transmitted by Jeff Forman from 4:33-6:53 am on September 21st, 2019. Typed & tweaked with minor revisions from 12:05-3:00 am on September 26th, 2019. ALL RIGHTS RESERVED.

Inspired by and written directly after watching the season 5 episode of Stargate SG-1 #106 Menace underscoring my overall rejection & revulsion to modern technology & my perception of the apparent addiction and enslavement of much of humanity in their apparent ignorance of its innate perils!

ILLICIT PROFITS IMMORALLY GARNERED AT WHAT COSTS BY THOSE WHO ARE SPIRITUALLY LOST!

Our early years imprint upon us many thoughts
which can shape our destiny with untold costs.
Some yield tears that stint compassion sought,
That ditch in place sours testimony for boldness bought!
Comes fields of fear which steer dispassioned actions wrought
which pitch some fakes with empowered takes
leaving many overwrought!

And thus the game remains the same
for those whose justifiable claim to income gained,
breaks those meek who've cowered,
their holdings subsequently greedily devoured!
These predators come in many shapes and sizes,
But some of the most insidious exist within respectable guises!
Yet actually their postures retained fostered ill gotten gains
With untold stains upon their souls as
they've relinquished control
of accountability to the edicts of morality and stability of ethics!
Which should never be sacrificed on the alters of inflexible laws
empowered at their expense,
For the damage done from such claws
of perverse duality is truly immense!

Producing only more laundered moles and trolls
Who've sidelined their high selves to the knell of usurped reason,
content to feather themselves tarred with unprovoked treason!

Resulting in much grievin' from those left alive who strive,
but find themselves unable to thrive
within the gullies of their grief
which sometimes becomes relinquished in defeat to their deceit.

It's enough to confound many
when a paid to play murderer makes a living
solely based upon anothers self centered immorally based giving,
But makes no excuses for their cold blooded lack of caring
and absent respect for others rights to live in the light
and ultimate grace of God's creation with elation
for all being created equal!

Yet how can we ignore and snore through
predatory banks that raise their steeples to supposedly nurture
a vested growth fostered in enriching society, when their piety
has been squandered fleecing the sheeple
with untold, illicit greed
for generations of Rothschilds and Rockefellers,
who've funneled their blood money into countless wars!
Funding both sides fomenting the bloodshed and violence,
steeped in the ongoing stench and the silence
of those entrenched in their vile stains of corruption!
Still yet apparently exempt from prosecution
or accountability, deemed
Too Big To Fail much less jail in the debacle of the 2008 bailout!
When many irate, fully awake and horrified
by this ongoing mistake,
again found morality displaced!

Shafted by graft fueled tyranny, and the ongoing societal aches
wrought by milking and bilking the people worldwide,
Unified in their quest to not be denied in finally driving
a stake through the cold hearts of these central bank vampires,
Whose stench of corruption is so vast and immense
That their entombment is a must, if the thrust of our society
can ever dispel its crust and be entrusted once again
to a sane and prosperous course for us all!
Where resources are shared to the enrichment of all,
and not stockpiled and squandered by a select few
in apparent power who seek to devour all!
If not struck down and forever entombed in unhallowed ground
laid forever to rest in the archaic annals of a perverse history!

Where once and for all humanity's divested itself of the worst
predatory perversion to ever curse its existence, also wrought by
elite families who have basked in immunity
from apparent impunity,
Aligned with orchestrating this illusion over countless
generations as a malicious intrusion upon the rights
of many, who've faithfully pursued paths of righteousness!
Seeking prosperity in meritorious service to all of their sisters
and brothers in deferential respect to the dignity of us all,
That we stand together united or divided we fall!

Yet we will never ever again allow ourselves to be tethered
in bondage to any that will fully promote gain,
Sullied with the sacrifice of many to an elite few,
Who will soon rue the day with chagrined dismay,
that they ever allowed themselves to stray
to the degree of their own souls betrayment
to justify enslavement!

Conceived and transmitted by Jeff Forman from 1:45 pm-4:00 pm on October 27th, 2019. Typed and tweaked with minor revisions from 10:45 pm Oct. 29th,- 1:00 am OCT. 30th, 2019.

Titled at 1:05 am October 30th, 2019. ALL RIGHTS RESERVED.

With minor revisions early am Nov. 12th, and early pm Nov. 13th, 2019 when it was reformatted. Inspired and written just after viewing The Big Valley #95 The Profit and The Lost (12/2/68).

THE SPURS OF GRIEF INDUCING TEMPORARY INSANITY CURED WITH COMPASSION RESTORING OUR OVERRIDING HUMANITY

Profound grief can drive us into displacing our humanity
with temporary insanity!
As some try to play God in order to re-stack the odds
into what they perceive their favor
To compensate for loss deemed unjust
by those perceived more famed they now mistrust
Who rigged the game in order to promote
their own material gains
for wealth they received as they dealt an unfair hand
In wielding their oppressive command
While others grieved at the expense of their loved ones
some of whom sadly perished mining the land!

As events can unfold in the aftermath,
Fate presents choices to which we can lend our voices
In support of seeking the truth or remaining aloof
to contort untold tainted sense
Away from actions founded in benevolence
which are purely heaven sent!
With such misalignment we resign ourselves
to become unwitting pawns who prolong deception
In contrast to cogent correction
to maintain the scales of justice refraining from malice,
Thus attaining clarity with actions steeped in charity
as we drink from a chalice of providential purpose!

Unified in unbiased service to all,
despite apparent pitfalls which often ensnare us,
As loss can frequently weaken us to easily default to cross
as we succumb to sadness
with countenances bleak opposed to exhibiting gladness.

Can we compose ourselves enough,
Even integrating self bluff to overcome our anger
to be shelved as we delve more into ourselves
to reach our souls connection with proper reflection
Away from self deception back to source
as a reservoir of resource!
To reengage our internal sage, quieting our rage
Thus altering our course saving us from rash actions taken
which would only yield more pain in vain without refrain?

Yet we must not view our negative emotions with disdain,
But learn to embrace their perceived unwelcome,
uncomfortable thrust into our lives
Without conniving to circumvent the extent of our pain
which can be cauterized,
When we face it compassionately with heartfelt healing
directed within as well as without
Quelling the knell of our fraught feelings
which in anguish have sent us reeling!

We should never allow quick impulses
to hedge our bets backing anything less
Than wise forethought exerted
leveraging any desired results that might result in regrets!

For any such feedback loop contorting or distorting truth
must never be conveyed to further enslave us
to additional prolonged staid emotions or further dread.

Instead we must yearn to learn to apply lotions
easing any aggravating commotions
resulting from our exasperated emotions,
With pleasing devotions in abundant supply and never denied,
With judicious insight always retained for what's rightfully gained
even for those wielding unjust might prone to fight
or in flight from the light!
So delight's the norm when returning to form,
Retaining the dignity of ubiquitous benignity!

Conceived and transmitted by Jeff Forman from 3:04-4:54 am with last line added 6:00-6:03 am
on October 29th, 2019. Tilted at 5:00 am. ALL RIGHTS RESERVED. Inspired and written immediately
following viewing The Big Valley episode #102 The Twenty-Five Graves of Midas (February 3rd, 1969).
Typed and tweaked with a few additions and revisions from 7:50- 9:50 pm on October 29th, 2019.

Printed in the United States
By Bookmasters